Contents

Materials & Techniques 180

CONTAINER
GARDENING

250 Design Ideas & Step-By-Step Techniques

From the EDITORS and CONTRIBUTORS
of *FINE GARDENING*

The Taunton Press

The Taunton Press
Inspiration for hands-on living®

The Taunton Press, Inc.
63 South Main Street
PO Box 5506,
Newtown, CT 06470-5506
e-mail: tp@taunton.com

Editors: Carol Kasper, Jen Matlack
Copy editor: Karen Fraley
Indexer: Lynda Stannard
Cover design: Teresa Fernandes
Interior design: Susan Fazekas,
    Teresa Fernandes
Layout: Susan Fazekas, Teresa Fernandes
Plant diagrams: Tinsley Morrison

Library of Congress Cataloging-in-Publication Data
Container gardening : 250 design ideas & step-by-
step techniques / editors, Carol Kasper, Jen Matlack.
    p. cm.
 Includes bibliographical references and index.
 ISBN 978-1-60085-080-6 (alk. paper)
1. Container gardening. 2. Gardens--Design.
3. Plants, Potted. I. Kasper, Carol. II. Matlack, Jen.
 SB418.C665 2009
 635.9'86--dc22

                    2008036238

Printed in the United States of America
10 9 8 7 6 5 4 3 2 1

The following manufacturers/names appearing in
Container Gardening are trademarks:
Angelface®, Babywing®, Cataline®, Diamond Frost®,
Dragon Wing™, English Butterfly Peacock™, Fusion™,
Kalipso™, New Wonder®, Snowstorm®, Snowstorm®
Giant Snowflake®, Superbells®, Supertunia®, Sweet
Caroline®, Sweet Heart Light Green™, Sweet Heart
Purple™, Tinkertoys®, Tukana®, Whirlwind®, Wilt-
Pruf®, Wink™

Large cover photo

1. **'Clear Skies' hebe**
   Hebe 'Clear Skies', USDA

2. **'Sundance' Mexican orange blossom**
   Choisya ternata 'Sundance'

3. **'Rhea' mealycup sage**
   Salvia farinacea 'Rhea'

4. **Urn gum**
   Eucalyptus urnigera

5. **'Silver Onion' echeveria**
   Echeveria 'Silver Onion'

6. **'Bella Mix' flowering maple**
   Abutilon x hybridum 'Bella Mix'

7. **'Ogon' sedum**
   Sedum makinoi 'Ogon'

8. **Golden creeping Jenny**
   Lysimachia nummularia 'Aurea'

Great Designs

A colorful hibiscus forms the apex of this three-sided composition, but pottery plays the starring role. Three exceptionally well-chosen containers, clustered together, with the smaller ones slightly to the fore, make a satisfying geometric pattern.

The Basics of Grouping Plants

BY SYDNEY EDDISON

GARDENING IN CONTAINERS CAN BE AS SIMPLE as filling a pot with a plant and placing it in a desirable spot. Chances are even this quick bit of work will produce a splash of color that enhances its location. But in container gardening, as with many worthwhile things, a little bit of forethought goes a long way. Whether you are composing a single pot or a grouping of pots that amounts to a small garden, using a triangular arrangement produces fast and pleasing results. Translated into the language of design, a triangle consists of a dominant central element flanked on either side by components of lesser stature. The triangular form is a staple of all art forms and for good reason: It always works.

Thus, a triangular composition using three containers of different heights, sizes, and shapes has everything to recommend it. The number is manageable, and the floor plan can be flexible. Triangles can be configured to fit any situation.

Your grouping will quickly fall into place if you set the tallest container in the apex of the triangle, with the other two pots on either side. Plant the tall container with something appropriately commanding, and allow it to dominate the composition. The other two containers and the plants they house can offer contrast in height and shape.

BELOW: The pleasure of this arrangement of pots is, of course, the imaginative use of a skeletal table of wrought metal. The rectilinear design ensures a strong sense of order, which is delightfully at odds with the unusual collection of plants. But even in this unconventional display, an underlying triangular framework can be detected, with the vertical leaves of the aloe supplying the high point.

FACING PAGE TOP LEFT:
Even four containers can be arranged to form a triangle. Here, the three smaller ones are placed around the base of the fourth and largest. Although the satellite pots are almost identical, one is given prominence over the other three simply by raising it up on stacked bricks.

FACING PAGE TOP RIGHT:
A profusion of purple and green foliage bursting from containers guarantees a successful grouping, no matter how many pots comprise the classic triangular motif.

LEFT: An irregular triangle in outline, this complex grouping includes a large number of pots, great and small, as well as a plant stand and a whimsical metal sculpture. The soft background of ornamental grasses creates an interesting textural foil for the composition of cacti, succulents, and man-made objects.

There's nothing to say that all the pots should be planted, either. An empty container with an interesting shape can be the making of a composition (photo, p. 4) or even serve as the focal point in a grouping (photo, above).

To expand a classic grouping, or to make it more complex, simply add more subordinate pots. There are no hard and fast rules about how many pots make a satisfactory combination. However, it is always easier to arrange uneven numbers into pleasing patterns. Groups of pots filled with flowers and lush foliage can greatly enhance man-made structures. Additionally, the lines and contours of the containers themselves create structure, which is a welcome contrast to natural forms.

An intriguing combination of plants, containers, and objets d'art guides visitors to this entrance. Grouped on either side of the doorway, the various elements are held together by a unifying theme of natural materials: wood, rusted metal, and living plants.

Create Welcoming Entryways

BY SYDNEY EDDISON

FLOWERS AND GREENERY AT AN ENTRYWAY SUGGEST that a warm reception awaits visitors within your home. But before you choose containers and plants for your entrance, consider the period and style of your house. Although you can work against an architectural style to exciting effect, it is much safer and easier to go with the flow. For example, familiar plants, traditional containers, and a symmetrical arrangement suit the clean lines of a Georgian colonial.

In choosing containers, also keep in mind the building materials used in the house and surrounding hardscape. The mellow hues and matte finish of terra-cotta pots go with almost any material but seem particularly at home next to brick or weathered wooden structures (photo, facing page). The neutral gray of cement or reconstructed limestone goes with everything and almost matches granite.

Often, potted plants at entryways serve practical as well as esthetic purposes, such as identifying the main entrance of a house with multiple outside doors. A pair of attractive containers can spare visitors confusion by leading the way to the appropriate door. Finally, plants at the entryway create a transition between the house and the natural world, bringing the garden right up to the door.

ABOVE: If you happen to miss the purple door, which is unlikely, a pair of stone acorns surrounded by an imaginative collection of plants will catch your attention, make you smile, and bid you welcome.

LEFT: The charm of this entryway lies in its simplicity and the suitability of the floral decoration. As befits an old gray-shingled cottage, the friendly, familiar pink impatiens lead you straight up the steps to the front door.

Potted plants bring the garden to the doorstep of this house, enhancing the elegant glasswork at its entrance. Soft, rounded plant forms and an abundance of bright flowers contrast with the linear patterns and restrained colors of the architecture.

Even a gallon or two of still, dark water attracts the eye like a magnet. Simple and compelling, these two containers draw the visitor down the garden path to mystery and adventure

Create Boundaries and Direct Traffic

BY SYDNEY EDDISON

I T'S AMAZING WHAT A GROUP OF POTTED PLANTS CAN do. Tall, impressive plants in large containers can build walls where none exist, create privacy by enclosing open spaces, lead visitors along paths chosen by the gardener rather than by chance, and steer people clear of obstacles or sudden changes in level. Think of potted plants not only as decoration but also as movable partitions with many uses. Walls made with containers can be uninterrupted and hedgelike, or sketchy and permeable to sight.

Depending upon the degree of enclosure desired, gardeners can use potted plants to different effect. The deck shown in the top photo on p. 17 is only partly enclosed, with a gregarious arrangement that affords

views out into the landscape. The dining area on my terrace, however, is completely surrounded by an impenetrable jungle of plants, offering a place of quiet seclusion (bottom photo, p. 14).

Containers can serve a practical function as well. Lacy bamboos grown in two huge, handsome containers act as a border to keep visitors from inadvertently stepping off a side porch (photo, p. 15).

Paths make it possible to move through a garden with purpose, which may be as practical as arriving at a given destination or as impulsive as a sudden desire to wander. In either case, carefully sited containers can make the route

more appealing while indicating the way. Sometimes a straight path and a paved surface serve best. But for the meandering type, roads that twist and turn beckon with the promise of unexpected pleasures.

Containers can provide beautiful guidance, too. In the photo on the facing page, a stone pot doubles as a water feature, causing visitors to pause before descending the steps. There, a second pot indicates a change in direction.

In another garden, a narrow, zigzag path lures the curious into a maze of succulents planted in cylinders of metal and terra-cotta (top photo, p. 14).

RIGHT: Who could resist entering into the confines and the spirit of a garden with a zigzag path? Filling in the angles with spiky succulents in swirling, upright containers was a stroke of great ingenuity. The feeling of motion hurries visitors along, but the twists and turns in the path delay departure from this enchanted space.

BELOW: The dense, wraparound walls of colorful flowers and foliage completely enclose this dining area and create a secret garden from an otherwise open, exposed slab of concrete.

Pots of bamboo form a barrier substantial enough to prevent an accidental fall but airy and graceful enough to charm visitors. In addition to serving a practical purpose, they beautifully illustrate an artistic principle: the attraction of opposites.

ABOVE: Bright, bouncy colors, lots of open space, and a semi-permeable wall of containers give this deck a party-time atmosphere.

LEFT: Potted plants can both divide and connect different garden areas. Here, standard fuchsias in matching containers separate a green corridor of lawn from the rest of the garden and lead the way to a formal garden space with a sculptural centerpiece.

FACING PAGE: Nothing is more peaceful at the end of the day than to sit beneath an arbor and admire the garden. Here, smooth paving facilitates the approach to such a seating area between hedges of potted plants.

Without the curvaceous juniper, this elegant archway would be austere to the point of severity. Instead, the spiral-patterned tree breaks up the plain wall, repeating the S-curves in the ironwork and relieving the value contrast between black and white with green, needlelike leaves.

Break Up Wall Space

BY SYDNEY EDDISON

IN THE ARCHITECTURE OF THE 18TH AND 19TH CENTURIES, a pleasing balance existed between walls and windows. Homes were typically smaller than they are today, and their simple facades had openings for a door or doors and a number of windows, all of which were harmonious in size and proportion to the amount of wall space. Where there were once barns and stables, now there are attached garages with expansive blank walls and huge openings to admit cars.

Changes in the way we live and do business have altered the function and look of both private homes and commercial buildings. In both, large, uninterrupted walls of glass, metal, masonry, or wood are now common. Some of these walls are just boring; others are downright ugly; a few are beautiful, depending on the material with which they are constructed. All cry out for pattern and the softening influence of leaves and blossoms. However, there are often problems associated with growing plants in close proximity to walls—insufficient room or inhospitable conditions such as lime in the soil leeched from foundation cement.

But there is a simple solution to all these challenges. Potted plants can be easily placed wherever needed. Unadorned walls, either of a building or freestanding, benefit from being broken up into smaller units. Plants are particularly effective in this role. They not only offer a broad spectrum of sizes, shapes, forms, and colors to create patterns of light and dark against a neutral background but also add movement. Small trees with diminutive leaves that flutter in the lightest breeze throw delightful shadows against a plain background.

ABOVE LEFT: The extravagant shower of angels' trumpets blossoms with nasturtiums at their feet makes such an eye-catching sight that the blank wall behind them disappears. Flowers and foliage in an assortment of containers relieve the otherwise dull expanse of wall.

ABOVE RIGHT: An attractive wire plant stand, a window box overflowing with pink geraniums, and an ornamental metal cross transform the narrow brick wall between these garage doors into a thing of beauty.

Unadorned with plants, this white wall would dominate with glaring brightness. But it is perfect as the background for a dense, complex arrangement of forms and colors. The plain surface sets off the rich hues and interesting leaf shapes, and the plants return the favor by creating patterns against the simple backdrop.

A beautiful effect was achieved here with the simplest possible means: large, good-looking pots containing small trees, evenly spaced along the entire length of a perfectly plain masonry wall. A border of fine-textured ornamental grass reinforces the line created by the trees so that together they hold their own against the solid mass of wall.

Think of a blank wall as a canvas, or what artists sometimes call a "support," for the medium of living plants. If you don't know how to create a pattern with containers, start with one of the classic groupings: three potted plants of different sizes arranged in a triangle. Soon you will see uninterrupted wall space not as a problem but as an opportunity to try new container compositions.

LEFT: The sandy texture of adobe bespeaks its earthy origin, and the soft, roseate hue goes with everything. Although an adobe wall needs no embellishment, it shows off plants and objets d'art to perfection. Here, blue wooden pot supports make a stunning contrast to the rosy-orange wall.

BELOW: In the absence of plants, the rigid, repetitive pattern of brick and mortar can be tiring to the eye. But when blurred by lush trailing foliage and colorful flowers, the lines of mortar recede. Here, the warmth of the brick is echoed by terra-cotta pots. Bright red blossoms bring the whole scheme to life and contrast with the greens of the foliage.

A colorful collection of potted plants buffers a sharp corner where two sections of wall meet. The wall returns the favor by elevating a double scarlet impatiens to star status and serving as a background where other plants flaunt brightly colored leaves and blossoms.

Use Pots to Soften Edges and Corners

BY SYDNEY EDDISON

SINCE MOST HOUSES ARE MADE UP OF CUBES AND rectangles, with outbuildings and garden structures that repeat geometric themes, corners abound. These right angles are, of necessity, sharp edged and project aggressively into the natural world. By arranging potted plants around outside corners, you can soften and blend these forceful angles into the landscape. And inside corners, which would otherwise be dead or wasted space, come wonderfully alive as settings for containers.

Old houses usually have a comfortable relationship with the land on which they sit and require no more than a couple of steps to reach the front door. But builders today have to make do with more and more difficult sites and dramatic changes in grade. Flights of steps have become an essential part of the system that links one level to another. Unadorned, a rigid pattern of treads and risers has an industrial look. Bank the same steps with potted plants and you've created a charming approach to the next platform.

Of course, edges are necessary and do play a vital role in defining and containing space, but their precision and sharpness can intrude upon our sensibilities. Even the edge of a well-built wooden planter or a gracious stone urn is often improved by a veil of leafy stems. Trailing plants blur hard lines and enliven inert containers. Less agreeable materials, such as plastic, can be covered by a lush living curtain.

An inside corner is less intrusive than an outside corner, but it's an awkward space nevertheless. Here, bushy coleus fill the angle between two panels of lattice. With its attractive openwork pattern and neutral gray tone, the lattice has a natural affinity for plants.

LEFT: Luxuriant geraniums, heliotrope, and licorice plant make a massive flight of stone steps appealing. The plants, spilling over the edges of their containers, mitigate the hard lines and edges of the treads and risers and soften the right angle where wall and ground meet.

BELOW: Significant changes of level require special treatment to ease the transition, such as using a system of steps and landings, retaining walls, or both. Here, plants reach to the edges of the wall, and a large, leafy specimen fills an inside corner, proving that where nature meets architecture, harmony can reign.

ABOVE: A few small plants and a delicate mat of silver foliage are all that it takes to camouflage the sharp lines of tread, riser, and wall. Tucked in the corner where a single step intersects with a wall, one container does the job.

RIGHT: The size, stature, and graceful form of this plant-filled urn are tailor-made for the corner that it commands, and the planting matches the elegance and simplicity of the container. Trailing variegated ivy softens the edge without in any way detracting from the urn's attractive shape.

ABOVE: The waterfall of silver licorice plant *(Helichrysum petiolare)* enhances a decorative wooden planter by disguising the hard edge. Continuing its downward course, the soft foliage will eventually flow across the pavement.

LEFT: A blanket of Swedish ivy conceals a plastic window box set on a low brick wall. The trailing stems, covered with abundant green and white leaves, cascade down to the surface of the terrace.

A comely purple container adds a theatrical accent to a garden already full of interest and excitement. Bold but not brash, the startling color is reflected in the gazing balls and picked up by allium blossoms and geranium leaves.

Create Drama with Focal Points

BY SYDNEY EDDISON

A N EYE-CATCHING OBJECT, LIKE A SINGLE distinguished container, can provide a garden with high drama. These focal points are often found at the end of a long vista or as the centerpiece of a garden divided into quadrants. The function of a focal point is to draw our eye and arouse and then satisfy our interest. But a pot or urn must be in scale with its surroundings, and, in a very large garden, it may need the reinforcements provided by other pots. For example, the garden shown in the top photo on p. 35 would prove too much to handle even for the massive container, appropriately elevated and extravagantly planted, were it not for the supporting cast. In this case, a low basin of succulents in the foreground and a pair of empty urns at the top of the steps are the cast members that maintain our interest and lead our eyes onward and upward to the star of the show.

A garden is most satisfying, though, when there is a beginning, middle, and an end, with excitement throughout that builds to the climax. Accents create these moments of excitement or heightened interest. An accent, whether it is a stressed syllable or a carefully placed pot, is about emphasis, and emphasis often is achieved by contrast. Thus, a striking container nestled in a bed of hosta, ferns, and nasturtiums offers a solid form that contrasts with the soft foliage and flowers (bottom photo, p. 35). A focal point provides the finishing touch to a garden picture; an accent adds a grace note that enriches the scene without dominating it.

As a decorative addition to the garden, no item has enjoyed a longer history than the container. While there may be such a thing as too many pots, one well-chosen container can make a powerful statement.

ABOVE: What could be simpler than a pot of brilliant cerise flowers set off by a gray wooden wheelbarrow? In fact, it is an artful, stunningly successful device to draw the eye. As a backdrop, the narrow cone of an evergreen completes a classic triangle, creating a thoroughly satisfying picture.

FACING PAGE TOP: Traditional and beautiful, a fine pot marks the center and serves as the focal point of a formal garden. The height and understated elegance of the container perfectly suit its surroundings, as the pot quietly dominates the garden.

FACING PAGE BOTTOM: In this enclosed garden, a single container provides the focal point for a view of the inner sanctum and reflecting pool. Set apart by the space around it, the deep color of the container and its girth, rather than its height, support its claim as the most important position in the garden.

RIGHT: Focal points make the experience of gazing down the long axis of a garden worthwhile. Here, the reward at the far end of a patio is a large rounded container. Although a spiky plant nearby is slightly taller, the round centerpiece dominates the scene by virtue of its size, weight, and position, reinforced by an evergreen exclamation point in front of it.

BELOW: Another vessel worthy of stardom, this lovely terra-cotta jar serves as an accent at one stage of a garden journey that promises other pleasures and surprises.

LEFT: In a large garden filled with distractions, there is even more need to manage space and to control the eye. Narrowing this broad path as it approaches the visual climax accomplishes two things: It increases the sense of distance between the viewer and the brick column supporting the container, and it makes the towering container seem even more dramatic.

BELOW: When does a focal point become an accent? When it is tucked in among the plants lining a narrow stepping-stone path. To one side, rather than in the middle of the view, this gorgeous pot evokes admiration without delaying the garden visitor, who may then press on to discover what is around the next bend in the path.

To have this gorgeous view of the Empire State Building marred by a vent would have been unthinkable. Fortunately, a narrow trellis, a large flower pot, and hyacinth bean saved the day. Together they provide a leafy screen to hide the eyesore and contribute another upright silhouette to the vertical shapes of New York City.

Pots to Frame and Screen

BY SYDNEY EDDISON

A PAINTING ALMOST ALWAYS LOOKS BETTER placed within a frame. I reckon that if a painting is worthy of a frame, it's worthy of note—and a closer view. In the garden, framing selected subjects has a similar effect. By excluding some garden views and including others, we focus the picture and heighten its importance. In the wider landscape, controlling the field of vision is most often assigned to evergreen hedges or other structural plantings, but there is no reason not to use potted plants in the same way.

How you frame a garden view depends on the subject; it may be as expansive as a distant prospect or as intimate as a birdbath. When the picture is a landscape, make the frame tall enough and substantial enough to hold its own with the view. Container gardeners devise ingenious ways to gain the necessary height and substance. One possibility is to group together bold structural plants. Another tactic is to attain height by stacking empty pots to form matching towers (top photo, p. 39).

For a quick approach to framing, install a ready- or custom-made arch. Flank it with potted plants and voilà! The result provides instant gratification. Take the use of an arch to another level by setting containers on either side and planting vines in each. It only takes annual vines a few weeks to smother an arch with foliage and flowers. The result is softer and less formal, but it serves the same purpose: to offer the viewer a pleasant scene contained within a decorative border.

Screening is the flip side of framing. In the suburbs, we need to camouflage downspouts and railings and tuck garbage cans out of sight. For urban dwellers with

rooftop or patio gardens, drains, vents, the barbecue on an adjacent terrace, and the walls of nearby buildings can be eyesores.

While suburbanites find numerous ways to conceal ugliness with in-the-ground plantings, city dwellers are limited in their options. However, if they become container gardeners, their troubles are over. Enter lattice and potted plants—what a dynamic combination! Affix a section of lattice to a planter, sow some hyacinth beans, and soon, a thick, leafy curtain will block out undesirable bits of the urban environment. Selective concealment is the name of the game, and it can be readily done with containers and their occupants.

ABOVE: An interesting arrangement of loquat, hebe, and sedge, planted in a good-looking container, partially conceals that inelegant necessity, a downspout.

LEFT: A wooden frame, wreathed in dainty clematis, contains a picture that could be characterized as Victorian with a twist. Wrought-metal furniture harks back to the turn of the last century, as do many of the tropical plants, but the informal arrangements of containers and the robust palette reflect a modern sensibility.

ABOVE: Here, the field of vision has been controlled in a strikingly original manner with matching towers of terra-cotta pots. As a base, the stacked pots have enough bulk to support large urns that, in turn, provide the necessary height to frame the deep garden vista.

LEFT: A rich tapestry of hyacinth bean and clematis screens out a metal fence and the wall of the building next door. The plantings furnish a delightful background for the planter, which contains a combination of small shrubs and perennials. Potted plants complete the garden picture in this urban oasis.

This big-leaved golden fruit of the Andes grows so quickly that staging it on different raised levels through the season ensures it remains the star of the display.

Staging a Display

BY STEVE SILK

I GROW PLANTS IN POTS BY THE SCORE IN A SPRAWLING garden of containers arranged like a border on my patio. By early summer, this arrangement of annuals, tender perennials, and the odd hardy plant has become an extravaganza of texture, fragrance, and color. To keep things lively as the plants grow, I simply move the containers—farther apart, up, down, to the front, to the rear—to create a display that is always evolving.

The portability of plants in pots frees me from some of the constraints of traditional earthbound gardening. It gives me the flexibility to tweak my jungle all season, adding bits of color as something new comes into prominence or removing anything that's past its prime.

Although I take a more-is-merrier approach to container gardening, numbers alone don't mean much. Five pots are enough to create a dramatic composition on a porch or patio. The trick is not how many pots you have but what you do with them. And for raising my container garden's beauty to new heights, the use of simple staging—by which I mean the overturned nursery pots, bulb crates, logs, and homemade plant stands that give plants and ornaments a boost—has been the greatest trick of all.

Use staging to create drama

By placing short but stellar plants atop staging that's hidden amid other plants, I can create compelling combinations that wouldn't be possible with plants grown in the ground. I especially like a combination of rubylike tropical smoke bush foliage and the coral-colored flowers of *Fuchsia* 'Coralle'. Unfortunately, the euphorbia is about 4 feet tall and the fuchsia a mere 2 feet. But by giving the fuchsia a boost on a foot-tall support, I can unify the two, adding a few coleus—also piggybacked

Overturned Pots Play a Supporting Role

ANYTHING THAT IS STURDY and stable can be used as a support to elevate pots. Use overturned pots of various sizes to create subtle height differences (photo at left), with customized drip-irrigation (the black tubing in the photo below right) to meet the basic water and fertilizer needs of the plants. Favorite props can include sturdy black nursery pots, which hide behind other pots and plants to create a display on the patio every summer (below center) or a more decorative version that is as vibrant as the plants themselves (below left).

on stands of varied heights—to round out the combination.

I've also found that staging can be a real boon to creating color echoes in my container border. Coleus and dahlias, for example, seem made for each other since it's easy to find a coleus with colorful foliage to match the hue of almost any dahlia. But the dahlias I like are 3 to 4 feet tall, while few coleus top 30 inches. By giving the coleus a boost of a foot or two, their decorative foliage becomes a colorful companion to the dahlias' floral fireworks.

Staging is also a good way to make the most of fast-growing plants in a container display. Golden fruit of the Andes (*Solanum quitoense*), the big-leaved plant in the center of the display on page 40,

is a plant I love for its huge, furry, spiked leaves, but it grows so quickly it's hard to maintain it in a starring, close-up role. So, early in the season, I raise it on staging to a position of prominence, then as the plant grows, I move it to shorter platforms until finally, by late August, there's no need for any staging at all. Small, slow-growing plants as well as plants that display flowers with strong visual appeal or fragrance can also benefit from staging by bringing them closer to eye level.

Raise objects to eye level

Staging can also be an effective way to display ornaments such as small fountains, sculptures, or handsome empty pots (photo, p. 44). In a container garden,

Raise Containers on Pedestals

ONE OF THE EASIEST WAYS to add height and interest to your garden is by placing containers on top of tall concrete columns. Married together, the two will provide dramatic focal points and textural contrasts to the surrounding foliage and flowers. The elevated containers, with their simple but elegant plantings, offer yet another opportunity to play with color and form—both within the vessels themselves and in their relationship to the surrounding garden.

The smooth texture and neutral color of the pedestals contrast nicely with the lush plantings, making those features stand out and highlight the combinations they support.

it's easy to place ornaments where they look best, and with staging, the options are unlimited. I have a fountain of copper pots (photo, facing page), but it's only about 18 inches tall and would be immediately overwhelmed by a surround of abutilon, dahlias, and coleus. So I just piggyback the fountain on some staging, and it rises to a place of honor.

Almost anything can serve as a plant stand, provided it's tall enough to lift the plant to the desired height, stable enough not to topple in the wind, and sturdy enough not to collapse when the pot on top gets a heavy watering. I've found that heavy-duty black-plastic nursery pots—the kind that usually contain small trees or large shrubs—work well. Their only drawback is their rather limited range, typically 10 to 18 inches high. For something taller, I often use logs that measure a foot or so in diameter, cut to length.

For larger supports that will hold several pots at once, I sometimes use overturned bulb crates—the hard plastic containers used for shipping bulbs. If need be, they can be stacked one atop the other. I've also built benchlike stands using 2x10 or 2x12 pressure-treated lumber. All it takes is a length of lumber and two shorter pieces for legs.

This display of 'Kingwood Kritter' coleus, 'Wyoming' canna, and an unknown yellow dahlia changes throughout the season to highlight plants that are in bloom.

Setting the Stage

THE KEY TO VISUAL APPEAL is elevating plants to different heights, which is easy by using risers in a variety of heights. Potted plants placed in front of the risers hide them from view.

To further the illusion that some plants are of unusual height, I hide supports behind containers planted with sprawling lantanas or coleus, which act as a ground cover. For plant stands that will be visible, options include attractive concrete or ceramic supports available at many garden centers. In winter, I some-times retreat to my basement workshop to build plant stands out of pine lumber. I make them whatever height I want, embellish them with ornamental molding, then add a coat of paint. All of these supports give my garden a boost and give me the chance to jigger a border without digging anything up.

The foliage of these potted perennials—bleeding heart, lungwort, and spotted deadnettle—stays interesting throughout the summer, even after the plants have stopped blooming.

Using Perennials in Pots

BY CHRISTINE FROEHLICH

WHEN PRESENTED WITH THE ESTIMATE FOR THE list of annuals for containers on her terrace, my customer lamented, "It seems like so much money to spend on plants that will be thrown away at the end of the summer." Aiming to please, I decided to experiment with perennials that could be used in containers and later transferred to the garden.

Before this, I hadn't tried using any perennials in containers. At first, visions of flopping plants and pathetic foliage flashed through my head. What was I going to do about the fact that most perennials only bloom for about a month? I began looking through plant catalogs with a few requirements in mind.

Which plants to choose

First, I didn't want anything that had to be staked or fussed with. Then I looked for plants with interesting textures and colorful foliage. Finally, I wanted to be able to reuse these plants in the garden. Some of the plants had to be able to withstand the relentless heat and sun of a southwestern exposure. Others needed to flourish in the shady conditions of the north side of the house. The containers needed to be planted by mid-May and still look good by the end of the summer.

My choices for that first season were a bit cautious, but they were successful. For the sunny side, I chose groupings of fountain grass, tickseed, tricolor sage, and aster. Because I planted in early May, I decided to use the annual white alyssum to spill out over the edge of the container, to give it interest until the perennials kicked in. On the shady side, I used 'Frances Williams' hosta, bleeding heart, and spotted deadnettle, with the annual blue lobelia as an edging.

By the time I had finished, the containers looked respectably full, although a bit quiet. By mid-June, the perennials were so full that they almost covered up the alyssum and lobelia on the edges. The foliage colors of the hosta and lamium were cool and soothing on the shady refuge of the north-facing terrace, and the foliage of the bleeding heart lasted well into early fall. The tickseed beamed its pale yellow lights starting in July and was a handsome companion to the fountain grass. In August, when most containers are looking weary, mine were fresh and lively.

Transfer plants to the garden at season's end

The perennial containers were much easier to care for than their annual counterparts. They required far less deadheading and deadleafing than annuals do. I was able to water them less often, and they didn't get that tired look that annuals have around Labor Day. Also, I enjoyed watching the transition of the plants' growth throughout

TIP

Tips for Planting Perennials

- Pick a perennial that will be the dominant center and then choose at least two others with foliage and flowers that contrast or blend with your primary plant.

- Think first about foliage color because it will likely dominate the planter and determine which flowers best suit the design.

- Consider the ultimate size of the plants and make sure the plants won't overwhelm the container as they grow.

the season. This was a great way to experiment with new plants. I had all summer to note their habits and changes and to decide where and how I wanted to use them in the garden.

I emptied the containers in October. Even though they still looked pretty good,

Plants for Shade

Lady's mantle

Foam flower

Siberian bugloss

American maidenhair fern
Adiantum pedatum
ZONES: 3–8

Barrenwort
Epimedium spp. and cvs.
ZONES: 4–9

European wild ginger
Asarum europaeum
ZONES: 4–8

Foam flowers
Tiarella spp. and cvs.
ZONES: 3–9

Lady's mantle
Alchemilla mollis
ZONES: 4–7

Siberian bugloss
Brunnera macrophylla and cvs.
ZONES: 3–7

Blue oat grass

Lavender

Short fountain grass

Snow in summer

Spurge

Wormwood

Blue oat grass
Helictotrichon sempervirens
ZONES: 4–9

Bowles' golden sedge
Carex elata 'Aurea'
ZONES: 5–9

Bronze fennel
Foeniculum vulgare 'Purpureum'
ZONES: 4–9

Lavender
Lavandula spp. and cvs.
ZONES: 5–9

Michaelmas daisy
Aster novi-belgii 'Professor Anton Kippenberg'
ZONES: 4–8

Short fountain grass
Pennisetum alopecuroides 'Moudry', 'Little Bunny', and 'Hameln'
ZONES: 6–9

Snow in summer
Cerastium tomentosum and cvs.
ZONES: 3–7

Spurge
Euphorbia spp. and cvs.
ZONES: 4–11

Wormwood
Artemisia spp. and cvs.
ZONES: 3–9

I wanted the plants to have a chance to acclimate to the garden before the cold weather arrived. I carefully lifted the plants out using my trowel and hands. Some plants had grown quite a bit, so I divided them—an added bonus. I went around the garden with my "leftovers," tucking them into bare areas. Some plants didn't fit into the existing garden scheme just then, so I put them aside into a holding bed for the following year. I treated them all as new perennials, watering them well and covering them with evergreen boughs after the ground froze to protect them from heaving.

Originally, I had planned for my containers to be at their peak in August and September, but experimenting with perennials over the years has shown me that I can have a palette of color and texture that changes throughout the season.

The bold forms and textures of cacti and succulents are a perfect match for one-plant pots. Here, an urn of echeveria (*Echeveria* sp., Zones 10-11) rises above globes of barrel cactus (*Ferocactus* sp., not hardy below Zone 11) and a spiky mescal (*Agave parryi*, Zones 9-11)

Highlighting One Plant in One Pot

BY JUNE HUTSON

CONTRARY TO THE RELIABLE STRATEGY OF USING a plethora of plants in a single container, one plant in a pot can really shine. Placing just one plant in an urn or container enables it to achieve its full potential in size and vigor, which would be compromised if it were competing with other plants for space, light, and nutrients. There are many plants with unique attributes that can attract attention when standing alone. Consider the structure of shrubs like hydrangeas, which like to stretch out their branches in every direction, or plants like New Guinea impatiens with their tightly rounded habits. Featured singly in a container, these plants can impart a dramatic impact wherever they are displayed.

Choose plants for maximum impact

In a container that has many different plants, a failure is easy to hide. If one plant doesn't live up to its potential, the other plants can compensate and the container will still look presentable. If the pot has just one member, it had better be a good one. When searching for a perfect plant to fill a pot, look for long-lasting, attractive foliage; exceptional form; and perhaps an added bonus, like a long bloom period.

Cannas are a good example of plants to grow on their own. Beautiful but needy, they do not share water and nutrients well with pot mates. Large cultivars, such as 'Australia' or 'Pretoria', develop their rhizomes quickly, even in a container. They need all of the space a pot has to offer to produce their numerous stems of abundant flowers. Together with their bold leaves, they make a dramatic statement.

Like cannas, most shrubs grown in confined quarters need the entire soil mass of a pot to grow and produce flowers. Vigorous shrubs, such as butterfly bushes (*Buddleia davidii* and cvs., Zones 6–9), are much better grown alone in a pot as they quickly develop a mass of shoots and roots. Hydrangeas (*Hydrangea* spp. and cvs., Zones 4–9) exhibit a rounded form that looks so much better displayed alone.

The hardiness of a woody plant for a container is an important issue. Unless I know that I can move a container into a greenhouse or dig the shrub out of the pot for the winter, I always choose shrubs that are a zone hardier than recommended for my climate. Ideally, shrubs or trees are best moved to a spot close to a house or building, preferably on the east side so that they're sheltered from winter winds. You can pile the area around the pot with straw to provide an even cozier environment. It's also important that the pots you choose are made of materials that are resistant to winter damage, such as concrete, wood, resin, or plastic.

The restricted root area of a pot keeps some plants small, so the range of material for specimen plantings can be broadened to include plants that would grow larger in the ground. This is most evident when using ornamental grasses, shrubs, and trees. Ornamental grasses quickly become spectacular specimens in containers. Their inflorescences add grace and movement to the garden. Grasses such as *Panicum virgatum* 'Northwind' (Zones 5–9), with tall, blue foliage, mature to a smaller height when in pots. Fountain grasses (*Pennisetum alopecuroides* and cvs., Zones 6–9) perform well when confined, and they can remain outdoors for fall and into winter, giving you three seasons of interest. Shrubs such as winterberry (*Ilex verticillata* 'Red Sprite', Zones 5–8), redtwig dogwoods (*Cornus alba* and cvs., Zones 2–8), and red osier dogwoods (*Cornus stolonifera* and cvs., Zones 3–8) fill out a container nicely. They take a back seat to more colorful specimens during the summer, but in winter they light up dreary days with colorful berries or stems.

Matching a Plant to Its Pot

IT'S EASY TO GET CAUGHT up in standard design rules, but the truth is that you can match almost any plant shape with almost any pot shape as long as the scale is balanced. When a container suits its occupant, and vice versa, it just looks right. A plant's size usually dictates the size of the pot, but the shape of the pot is up to you.

TALL, NARROW POT
If a plant has a strong vertical habit, the look is intensified when put in a tall, narrow pot. Plants with a rounded habit placed in a tall pot may take on the appearance of a cone with a big scoop of ice cream on top.

SHORT, SQUAT POT
When a short, rounded pot is used for a plant with a strong vertical habit, it looks like it is anchored to the ground.

MEDIUM-SIZE POT
If the container is about the size of the expected mature size of the plant within, the combined shapes take on the look of a balanced composition.

LEFT: When planted in their own pots, plants can be moved around and arranged on a whim. This sedum and fountain grass make a pleasing pair in a courtyard.

BELOW: These bold, simple pots of Dragon Wing® Red begonias accent, rather than distract from, the matching front door.

Many annuals and perennials are good to grow singularly in pots as well. Annual impatiens quickly form a nicely rounded mound, bloom nonstop all summer, and can be grown in sun or shade. Begonia Dragon Wing® Red is one of the ultimate plants for a container. Its shiny foliage fills in quickly, and it blooms nonstop. It gets large by the end of the growing season, so a medium-size to large pot works best. Umbrella plant (*Cyperus alternifolius*, Zones 9–11) is great for a pot without a drainage hole because it needs constant moisture; it also adds an exotic look to any location. Perennials like *Hosta* 'Sum and Substance' (see photo, below center) and *H.* 'Golden Sculpture' (Zones 3–9) add bold drama to a shady patio with their chartreuse foliage.

Things to consider when matching a plant to a pot

Let the colors of both plants and pots help dictate your design. I particularly like the jewel colors of glazed ceramic pots as they can be a contrast to plants or an extension of the same hue. One of my favorite color-harmony combos is Cape leadwort (*Plumbago auriculata*, Zone 11) in a blue pot (see photo, below left). The plant's exuberant stems reach out in all directions, creating a tumble of blue flowers that mimic the same azure shade of the ceramic container in which it is planted. In addition to the color harmony, its wild form engulfs the pot just enough to create a living sculpture. A similar pairing is a short, dark purple pot planted with purple shamrock (*Oxalis regnellii* var. 'atropurpurea', Zones 7–10), which is basically the same shade as the container. The pairing of the shiny container surface with the sheen of the triangular purple leaves is outstanding.

A cobalt blue pot complements the azure blooms of Cape leadwort.

Plants with bold foliage, like this 'Sum and Substance' hosta, add drama to any location.

The wide, mounded forms of some plants, such as this blue anise sage, combine well with large, wide pots.

Great Plants for One-Plant Pots

ANNUALS AND TENDER PERENNIALS

Blue anise sage
Salvia guaranitica 'Black and Blue'
ZONES: 7–10

Cape leadwort
Plumbago auriculata
ZONE: 11

Chile pepper
Capsicum annuum cvs.
ANNUAL

Dahlberg daisy
Thymophylla tenuiloba
ANNUAL

Dragon Wing Red begonia
Begonia Dragon Wing Red
ZONE: 11

Elephant's ear
Colocasia esculenta and cvs.
ZONES: 8–11

Fiber optic grass
Isolepis cernua
ZONES: 8–10

Flowering maple
Abutilon spp. and cvs.
ZONES: 8–11

Impatiens
Impatien spp. and cvs.
ANNUAL

Tropical smoke bush
Euphorbia cotinifolia
ZONES: 9–11

Umbrella plant
Cyperus alternifolius
ZONES: 9–11

PERENNIALS AND GRASSES

Anise hyssop
Agastache foeniculum 'Golden Jubilee'
ZONES: 6–10

Black-eyed Susan
Rudbeckia hirta and cvs.
ZONES: 3–7

Chile peppers

Tropical smoke bush

Fountain grasses

Hardy geranium

Bigleaf hydrangeas

Fountain grass
Pennisetum alopecuroides and cvs.
ZONES: 6–9

Hardy geranium
Geranium 'Rozanne'
ZONES: 4–7

Hosta
Hosta spp. and cvs.
ZONES: 3–9

Joe Pye weed
Eupatorium maculatum 'Gateway'
ZONES: 5–11

Sedum
Sedum spectabile cvs.
ZONES: 4–9

Switchgrass
Panicum virgatum and cvs.
ZONES: 5–9

TREES AND SHRUBS

Bigleaf hydrangea
Hydrangea macrophylla cvs.
ZONES: 6–9

Colorado spruce
Picea pungens 'Foxtail'
ZONES: 2–8

Hornbeam
Carpinus betulus 'Fastigiata'
ZONES: 4–8

Mugo pine
Pinus mugo 'Mops'
ZONES: 3–7

Red osier dogwood
Cornus stolonifera 'Cardinal'
ZONES: 3–8

Sevenbark hydrangea
Hydrangea arborescens 'Grandiflora'
ZONES: 4–9

Winterberry
Ilex verticillata and cvs.
ZONES: 5–8

Here, matching pots of pansies (*Viola* x *wittrockiana* cv., Zones 8-11) adorn a sundial pedestal.

Another example is the reddish hue of a terra-cotta pot that serves as an anchor to the ground but becomes more of a focal point when combined with the rustic colors of *Sedum* 'Autumn Joy' (Zones 3–11). To capitalize on contrast, forest green ceramic containers are stunning when planted with anything orange or red, such as an annual red flowering tobacco (*Nicotiana alata* 'Nicki Red').

Another factor to consider when designing a one-plant pot is pairing the size and proportions of a plant with a complementary pot. In general, plants with a rounded habit are successfully paired with pots of low, chubby proportions. Blue anise sage (*Salvia guaranitica* 'Black and Blue', Zones 7–10, see photo, bottom right, p. 54), a great hummingbird plant, has an overall rounded form that looks stunning in a squat pot. The vertical effect of a larger, more upright pot can be enhanced by pairing it with a similarly shaped plant, such as a tropical smoke bush (*Euphorbia cotinifolia*, Zones 9–11), cannas, upright coleus, or grasses. Top a small, narrow pot with a spiky hat by choosing a plant such as fiber optic grass (*Isolepis cernua*, Zones 8–10) or an agave (*Agave* spp. and cvs., Zones 9–11, see photo, p. 50). The same look can be achieved with a larger narrow pot using fountain grass (*Pennisetum alopecuroides* 'Hameln', Zones 6–9). Ornate, flaring urns benefit from the blowsy habit of shrubs such as hydrangeas or flowering maples (*Abutilon* spp. and cvs., Zones 8–11), which add Victorian charm to a cottage-garden setting. Draping ferns, such as the foxtail fern (*Asparagus densiflorus* 'Myersii', Zone 11), also work well.

One-plant pots like these tulips (*Tulipa* cvs, Zones 4–8) can make a bold statement in a garden and, when used in multiples, can frame an entryway or architectural element.

Use one-plant pots in several ways

The intrinsic beauty of one specimen plant in a pot can be used as a focal point or as an accent, leading the eye to a direction or destination wherever the container is placed. For example, a parterre garden with symmetrical beds can be connected into a whole by directing the eye to a single-plant container in the center of the garden. And a series of containers placed by a doorway directs a visitor to the point of entry. Pots placed along a garden walk draw you forward, perhaps to discover that the path continues on to a farther destination.

The design of a one-plant pot can sometimes be determined by the intended placement of the container. Scale is a strong criterion. A large ornamental grass or shrub complements an expansive hardscape area such as a patio or pool deck. Repetition of that same planting can create a vertical accent along a fence or path that moves the eye along like a bouncing ball, giving it direction. Using a matched pair of conifers at a doorway provides symmetry and adds a sense of permanence to the entry, with the added benefit of being able to decorate the plants with lights for the holidays. If the entry is not obvious, the containers can help point the way.

This container is packed with drama, from the spiky foliage of helichrysum, dracena, and canna to the bold color of dahlia and zinnia.

One Pot, Many Plants

BY JUANITA NYE

I STOOD LOOKING AT THE EXPANSE OF DECKING THAT surrounds our pool area, and I knew that I had my work cut out for me. My mission was to soften the harsh lines of the hardscape. What better way to do that than with boldly planted pots? With a quick scan of the scene, it was evident that the four existing redwood containers were too small and in bad shape. I'm always up for a gardening challenge, however, so I dove right in.

My first action was to replace the redwood containers with large, sturdy concrete containers. Then, since I like a tropical look, I selected plants with bold, architectural shapes such as bananas, cannas, and dracenas and planted each pot to its maximum capacity. The result was bountiful, dramatic, jam-packed containers that spilled over with color and visual interest.

Planning the extravaganza

I find that the big, bold, leafy plants with various textures, colors, and habits are the most important element of my container gardens. My planting plans are based on successful designs I've used in the past, yet I'm always open to experimentation and serendipity.

Since I like my containers to be abundant, I choose plants that I know will perform well in tight quarters. Color is also a factor in my selection, and I try to choose two or three colors of flowering annuals that complement the core architectural plants in each container. I find a limited palette to be more harmonious, and it also makes the plant search

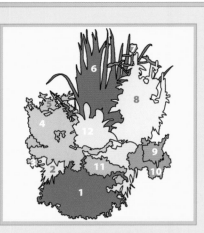

Hot Color Combo

1. **Lobelia**
   Lobelia ricardii
   ANNUAL

2. **Blue fescue**
   Festuca glauca
   ZONES: 4–8

3. **Snapdragon**
   Antirrhinum majus
   'Rocket Red'
   ANNUAL

4. **Blue bush sage**
   Salvia urica
   ZONES: 9–10

5. **Pitcher sage**
   Salvia azurea
   'Nekan'
   ZONES: 7–9

6. **Variegated iris**
   Iris cv.
   ZONES: 4–9

7. **Castor bean**
   Ricinus communis
   'Carmencita'
   ZONES: 9–10

8. **Giant hyssop**
   Agastache scrophulariifolia
   'Liquorice Blue',
   ZONES: 4–9

9. **Texas sage**
   Salvia coccinea
   'Lady in Red',
   ANNUAL

10. **Petunia**
    Petunia 'Azure Pearls'
    ANNUAL

11. **Petunia**
    Petunia 'Red Madness',
    ANNUAL

12. **Rubber plant**
    Ficus elastica 'Cabernet'
    ZONE: 11

much easier. I use hot colors in my tropical designs, and I've had great success with monochromatic color schemes as well as combinations that featured purple and red flowers; apricot and lavender flowers, and orange; yellow, and white flowers. I find the most difficult colors to work with are magenta and blue. I use all hues of the selected colors and choose plants with green, yellow, purple, and gray leaves to use as backdrops.

Getting the pots to thrive

For me, the ideal container size is 26 inches high and 30 inches across. I prefer using concrete pots because of their durability and unique sculptural qualities. I recommend drilling two ½-inch-diameter holes on each side of the con-

tainer, 4 inches up from the base, in addition to a drainage hole in the bottom. These unobtrusive holes, easily created with a masonry bit, not only allow for better drainage but also create a reservoir of water. If these side holes become obstructed, I poke them with a bamboo stake to allow the excess water to drain out.

Because my containers are packed with plants, the soil tends to become root-bound. So I begin each season with new soil—a mixture of compost, perlite, and 14-14-14 granular, slow-release fertilizer. Once the plants are in place, they flourish in their large-size containers as

Two Planting Methods

WHEN I FIRST STARTED container gardening, I brazenly packed each container with 30 plants. After several years, I have found more success using fewer plants, approximately 18 to 20 in each container. Annual plants sold in 4-inch containers, rather than in cell packs, are more apt to survive in crowded conditions since their roots systems are better developed. I always arrange the plants so they get the maximum exposure from the side they will be viewed from. I also pull out any plant that is not behaving. Here are two planting methods that I use when packing my large-size containers. Give both types of arrangements a long, slow soaking once plants are in place; this is especially important when using the alternate method to prevent soil runoff.

Plants in 4-inch-square pots or larger have more mature root systems and are more likely to flourish in a large, tightly packed container.

Standard Method

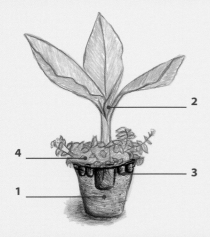

When my design calls for a hefty core plant I simply place the core plant near the center of the pot and pack in as many supporting plants as possible. Here are the steps I follow.

STEP 1:
Fill the container approximately halfway with fresh, damp soil and time-release fertilizer.

STEP 2:
Center the core plant slightly toward the back of the pot.

STEP 3:
Add more soil and time-release fertilizer to within 8 inches of the top of the container.

STEP 4:
Arrange the filler plants around the core plant, placing them as close together as possible and adding soil to secure each plant in place.

Alternate Method

When using a core plant with a smaller base or trunk I use an alternate planting method, which I've been experimenting with for the past few years. I like this method because it gives the core plant more height and creates more planting area for me to cram plants into. Here are the steps I follow.

STEP 1:
Fill the container approximately three-quarters full with fresh, damp soil and time-release fertilizer.

STEP 2:
Place the core plant in the center of the container, making sure the soil level of the plant sits approximately 2 inches above the top of the container.

STEP 3:
Add more soil and time-release fertilizer to the container to form a mound.

STEP 4:
Place filler plants as close together as possible into the mound so that they cascade over the edge of the container.

Foliage Adds Texture

1. Helichrysum
Helichrysum 'Icicles'
ZONES: 10–11

2. Sweet potato vine
Ipomoea batatas
'Margarita'
ZONES: 9–11

3. Zinnia
Zinnia
'Profusion Orange'
ANNUAL

4. Dracena
Dracaena sp.
ZONE: 11

5. Dahlia
Dahlia 'Snoho Wonder'
ZONES: 8–11

6. Canna
Canna 'Intrigue'
ZONES: 8–11

7. Petunia
Petunia 'Sonata',
ANNUAL

8. Alternanthera
Alternanthera dentata
'Rubiginosa'
ZONES: 9–11

Choose two or three colors of flowering annuals that complement the core architectural plants in each container.

long as I keep them well watered, either by a dependable automatic irrigation system or an unflagging hose handler. I also provide them with a weekly feeding of liquid fertilizer, and deadhead them regularly.

I keep a garden journal for each year's container design, devoting one page to each container and using a circle diagram to note the placement and name of each plant. I also attach a digital photo of the container to the page. The record keeping sounds tedious, but in the long run, it provides me with invaluable information. I learn which plants not only make good companions but also are easy to maintain and seasonally strong. It's taken some trial and error to learn which plants work best together, but that's part of the fun of growing plants in pots.

Big and Beautiful

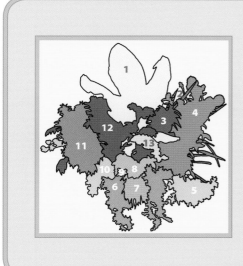

1. **Red banana**
   Ensete ventricosum
   'Maurelii'
   ZONE: 11

2. **New Zealand flax**
   Phormium tenax
   'Purpureum'
   ZONES: 9–10

3. **Oriental lily**
   Lilium 'Casa Blanca'
   ZONES: 4–8

4. **Dahlia**
   Dahlia 'Nicky K'
   ZONES: 8–11

5. **Dusty miller**
   Senecio viravira
   ZONES: 8–10

6. **English ivy**
   Hedera helix cv.
   ZONES: 5–10

7. **Blue fescue**
   Festuca glauca
   ZONES: 4–8

8. **Red bedding dahlia**
   Dahlia cv.
   ZONES: 8–11

9. **Salvia**
   Salvia splendens
   'Sizzler Burgundy'
   ANNUAL

10. **Bougainvillea**
    Bougainvillea 'Coral'
    ZONES: 9–11

11. **Lion's ear**
    Leonotis leonurus
    ZONES: 10–11

12. **Honey bush**
    Melianthus major
    ZONES: 8–10

13. **Stonecrop**
    Sedum spectabile
    'Meteor'
    ZONES: 4–9

Spectacular from the Start

1. **Coleus**
   Solenostemon scutellarioides 'Burgundy Wedding Train'
   ANNUAL

2. **Golden creeping Jenny**
   Lysimachia nummularia 'Aurea'
   ZONES: 4–8

3. **Mauritius hemp**
   Furcraea foetida 'Mediopicta'
   ZONES: 9–11

4. **Sweet potato vine**
   Ipomoea batatas 'Sweet Caroline Purple'
   ZONE: 11

Fabulous Foliage

BY FINE GARDENING EDITORS

GIVEN THE STAGGERING AMOUNT OF PLANTS WITH stunning foliage on the market these days, there are countless ways to create spectacular container designs that depend solely on interesting leaves—that's right, no flowers. Here are seven compelling designs that look good all summer long with minimal maintenance. There are also a number of options for shade. Down with deadheading!

Spectacular from the Start

The spiky green Mauritius hemp was the focus of this design created by Melonie Ice of Ada, Michigan. Chosen for its architectural form and mellow variegation, this beauty was as striking from just after it was potted to late in the season, when the other plants matured. The color scheme is a stunning accent to Melonie's beige-brick home, after which the pot's pedestal was fashioned. The hemp plant overwinters indoors so it can be used again the next spring.

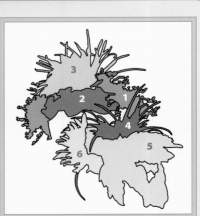

Bring on the Drama

1. **Creeping wirevine**
   Muehlenbeckia complexa
   ZONES: 8–10

2. **European ginger**
   Asarum europaeum
   ZONES: 4–8

3. **Variegated society garlic**
   Tulbaghia violacea 'Variegata'
   ZONES: 7–10

4. **Black mondo grass**
   Ophiopogon planiscapus
   'Nigrescens'
   ZONES: 6–11

5. **Rex begonia**
   Begonia cv.
   TROPICAL

6. **Sage**
   Salvia officinalis 'Nazareth'
   ZONES: 5–8

Bring on the Drama

Holly Shaffer of Kent, Ohio, created this
striking black-and-silver color combination
that lasted months after it was planted. This is
a good lesson in foliage-only containers—
plants that don't bloom can be tough, low
maintenance, and long-lasting, just like their
flowering countertops. The pot itself complements the foliage and doesn't compete with
the silvery tones.

A Pot as Inspiration

1. **Coleus**
   Solenostemon scutellarioides cv.
   ANNUAL

2. **Foxtail fern**
   Asparagus densiflorus 'Myersii'
   TROPICAL

3. **Heuchera**
   Heuchera 'Creme Brulee'
   ZONES: 4–8

4. **Persian shield**
   Strobilanthes dyerianus
   ZONES: 9–11

5. **Spike**
   Cordyline indivisa 'Purpurea'
   ZONES: 9–10

A Pot as Inspiration

Linda Brown really wanted to use her grand-mother's antique canning tub as a container but was afraid to ruin it. She found something similar in an antique store near her home in Coudersport, Pennsylvania, and used that as inspiration for two of the plants in this winning combination—the coppery heuchera and the bronzy spike. She fell in love with the foxtail fern at the nursery, and she chose the coleus and Persian shield to complement the other plants and round out her design.

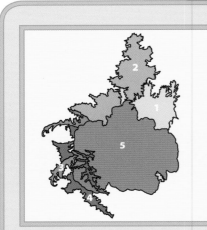

Sophisticated Silvers

1. **Curry plant**
   Helichrysum serotinum
   ZONES: 7–10

2. **Cypress**
   Cupressus sp.
   ZONES: 6–10

3. **Globe artichoke**
   Cynara scolymus
   ZONES: 8–9

4. **Licorice plant**
   Helichrysum petiolare 'Silver Mist'
   ANNUAL

5. **Silver sage**
   Salvia argentea
   ZONES: 5–8

Sophisticated Silvers

When the sidewalks outside Danny Ewert's house in Minneapolis were being renovated, he rescued a small cypress and popped it into one of his favorite pots. He surrounded it with silver sage and silver curry plant and artichoke, creating a design that focuses on texture within one color family.

A Thrilling Filler

This 'Escargot' begonia was the focus for this design created by Steve Nowotarski of Massapequa Park, New York. He chose plants that would fill in around the begonia but also add pizzazz on their own. The bright colors all blend together—even with the pot!—yet add their own drama as well.

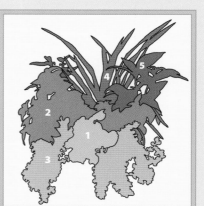

A Thrilling Filler

1. **Begonia**
   Begonia 'Escargot'
   TROPICAL

2. **Coleus**
   Solenostemon scutellarioides
   'Wizard Sunset'
   ANNUAL

3. **Licorice plant**
   Helichrysum petiolare 'Limelight',
   ZONES: 10–11

4. **Mountain flax**
   Phormium cookianum
   'Pink Stripe'
   ZONES: 8–11

5. **Persian shield**
   Strobilanthes dyerianus
   ZONES: 9–11

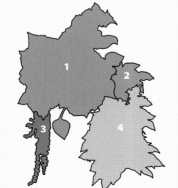

An Heirloom with a Twist

1. **Coleus**
   Solenostemon scutellarioides 'Kong Scarlet'
   ANNUAL

2. **Coleus**
   Solenostemon scutellarioides cv.
   ANNUAL

3. **Golden creeping Jenny**
   Lysimachia nummularia 'Aurea'
   ZONES: 4–8

4. **Sweet potato vine**
   Ipomoea batatas 'Chartreuse"
   ZONE: 11

An Heirloom with a Twist

Sheila Gamble's garden, in Olora, Ontario, is based mainly on foliage, with a common theme of burgundy, lime green, and deep green. The plants in this cast-iron urn, which dates back to the 1850s, fit into her color scheme; together plants and pot combine family history with flair.

Low Cost with Big Results

Not only don't you need flowers to create a lush container garden but you also don't need to spend a lot of money on a pot. Debra Corrington, who lives in Lexington, Virginia, recycled a garden-hose pot, which was the perfect size and had a generous drainage hole. Plants were chosen with an eye toward those that would survive the heat and humidity of a Virginia summer, combining an unlikely set of plants into a harmonious whole.

Low Cost with Big Results

1. **Golden elder**
   Sambucus racemosa
   'Sutherland Gold'
   ZONES: 3–7

2. **Heuchera**
   Heuchera 'Silver Scrolls'
   ZONES: 3–8

3. **Hosta**
   Hosta 'Stained Glass'
   ZONES: 3–9

4. **Snakeroot**
   Actaea simplex 'Brunette'
   ZONES: 4–8

5. **Variegated blue mist shrub**
   Caryopteris divaricata
   'Snow Fairy'
   ZONES: 6–9

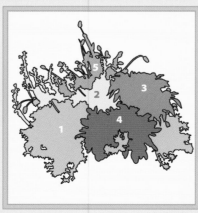

A Pepper of Many Colors

1. **Annual: Portulaca**
   Portulaca grandiflora
   'Sundial Orange'

2. **Perennial: Hyssop**
   Agastache aurantiaca
   'Apricot Sprite'
   ZONES: 7–10

3. **Vegetable: Sweet pepper**
   Capsicum annuum
   'Sweet Pickle'
   ANNUAL

4. **Herb: Purple sage**
   Salvia officinalis
   'Purpurascens'
   ZONES: 4–10

5. **Annual: Bunny tail grass**
   Lagurus ovatus

Incredible Edibles

BY FINE GARDENING EDITORS

A CREATIVE WAY TO EXPAND CONTAINER GARDENing horizons is by including plants that most gardeners would not think to plant in their pots. Tomatoes, artichokes, and onions, for example, may seem more at home in raised garden beds. But consider other possibilities. When planted in containers with other striking and unusual neighbors, vegetables can be delightful and dramatic. Here are 7 inventive container designs that look good enough to eat.

A Pepper of Many Colors

Wynn Young's container design was inspired by a sweet pepper called 'Sweet Pickle', whose peppers change color throughout the season from yellow to orange to red to purple. The rest of the plants harmonize with the colorful peppers and with each other. Wynn grew the bunny tail grass and hyssop from seed with the intention of planting them in her garden beds at her home in Rochester, Minnesota. But combined with purple sage and portulaca, a pot of many colors was created.

A Successful Collaboration

1. **Annual: Petunia**
   Petunia cv.

2. **Perennial:
   Pineapple mint**
   Mentha suaveolens
   'Variegata'
   ZONES: 6–9

3. **Vegetable:
   Artichoke**
   Cynara scolymus
   ZONES: 8–9

4. **Herb: Basil**
   Ocimum basilicum
   'African Blue'
   ZONES: 9–11

5. **Herb: Mealycup sage**
   Salvia farinacea
   ZONES: 8–11

A Chapeau for the Shade

Herbs and vegetables are typically part of containers created by Cheryl Thole, of Exeter, Rhode Island. Her site gets limited sunlight, and she reserves every bit of sun for her tomatoes. Cheryl focused instead on texture and color of shade-tolerant foliage plants for this container rather than on lots of flowers. The beet plant and pennyroyal look right at home with the annuals and perennials.

A Successful Collaboration

There's no such thing as too young to garden, and this container design proves the point. Ten-year-old Jackie Feigel of Novato, California, created this colorful pot with the assistance of her neighbor, garden designer Michelle Derviss. While Michelle provided some professional guidance, it was Jackie who used her own artistic eye to match the colors and textures of the plants.

A Chapeau for the Shade

1. **Annual: African daisy**
   Arctotis 'Sun Spot'

2. **Perennial: Hosta**
   Hosta 'Gold Standard'
   ZONES: 3–9

3. **Vegetable: Beet**
   Beta vulgaris ssp.
   cicla 'Bull's Blood'
   ANNUAL

4. **Herb: Pennyroyal**
   Mentha pulegium
   ZONES: 7–9

5. **Perennial: Purple
   fountain grass**
   Pennisetum setaceum
   'Rubrum'
   ZONES: 9–11

Letting It Flow

1. **Annual: Coleus**
   Solenostemon scutellarioides
   'Kiwi Fern'

2. **Perennial: Sedum**
   Sedum cv.
   ZONES: 3–9

3. **Vegetable:
   Red leaf lettuce**
   Lactuca cv.

4. **Herb: Basil**
   Ocimum basilicum 'Spicy Globe',
   ANNUAL

5. **Tropical: Begonia**
   Begonia 'Escargot'
   ZONE: 11

Growing Patio Vegetables

ANY KITCHEN-GARDEN plant can be grown in a container as long as you meet the plant's needs. All things being equal, container-grown plants mature at the same rate as those in the ground—sometimes sooner. As long as roots have ample room, any shape and any material may be used, although metal gets hot, as do containers in dark colors. The simplest soil mix—straight garden soil doesn't drain—is equal parts humusy garden soil, compost, sphagnum peat moss, vermiculite, and sharp sand. Place screening over the drainage holes to guard against slugs. Let the soil just dry out between waterings, and fertilize more lightly but more frequently than if the plants were in the ground.

Experiment with growing intensively; plant more vegetables to a pot than the label indicates. Be playful by mixing vegetables, fruits, herbs, and flowers. Half barrels make lovely mini gardens, provided all plants have similar requirements. And don't forget to hang a garden in baskets in the air: cherry tomatoes, Malabar spinach, and strawberries, for starters.

When planted in containers with other striking and unusual neighbors, vegetables can be delightful and dramatic.

Letting It Flow

Although Sally Wagoner of Chicago Heights, Illinois, drew her inspiration for this container design from the mounding shape of the 'Spicy Globe' basil, the other plants seemed to call out to one another. Sally combined coleus, sedum, and red leaf lettuce, focusing on texture, then on color, then on flow of the arrangement. The begonia caps it off.

White on white

Motria Caudill wanted to design a container that would stand out from the crowd, and this one does. She took a white-themed garden approach, choosing white acidanthera first, then selected plants with white or silver flowers, foliage or variegation to round out the recipe. Even the tomato is a variety that turns white as it matures.

White on White

1. **Annual: Dichondra**
   Dichondra argentea
   'Silver Falls'

2. **Perennial: Salvia**
   Salvia nemorosa
   'Snow Hill'
   ZONES: 5–9

3. **Vegetable: Tomato**
   Lycopersicon
   'Snow White'
   ANNUAL

4. **Herb: Tricolor sage**
   Salvia officinalis
   'Tricolor'
   ZONES: 7–8

5. **Annual:
   Acidanthera**
   Acidanthera cv.
   ZONES: 8–10

A creative way to expand container gardening horizons is by including plants that most gardeners would not think to plant in their pots.

A Homegrown Sweet Potato

1. **Annual: Million bells**
   Calibrachoa 'Superbells® White'

2. **Perennial: Wormwood**
   Artemisia 'Powis Castle'
   ZONES: 7–9

3. **Vegetable: Sweet potato**
   Ipomoea batatas
   ZONES: 9–11

4. **Herb: Lemon grass**
   Cymbopogon citratus

5. **Annual: Petunia**
   Petunia 'Purple Wave'

A Homegrown Sweet Potato

With sweet potato roots in hand (it took five tries to get a supermarket sweet potato to root in water!), Pam Watkins of Independence, Kansas, had the basis for a lush container. The antique washtub is home to the plants, with million bells, wormwood, lemon grass, and petunia completing the scheme.

Focus on Foliage

Foliage can be very dramatic, as evidenced here with the combination of glaucous foliate of a cabbage and the variegated foliage of a flowering maple. Keeping texture in mind, Holly Buss added cardinal flower and silver thyme, then added a punch of color with golden elder.

The Best Container Vegetables

There are so many great vegetables that can be grown in containers. Here are just a few.

1- to 2-gallon pots
- 'Touchon' carrots
- 'Evergreen White Bunching' scallions
- Shallots
- Garlic

3-gallon pots
- 'Tom Thumb' lettuce
- 'Golden' beets
- 'Cherry Belle' radishes
- Mustard greens
- 'Tokyo Cross' turnips

5-gallon pots
- 'Tiny Tim' cherry tomatoes
- 'Salad Bush' cucumbers
- 'Little Fingers' eggplant
- 'Miniature Red Bell' pepper
- 'Sugar Baby' watermelon

25-gallon Pots
- Burpee's 'Fourth of July' potato collection
- 'Oregon Spring' tomatoes
- 'Table Gold' winter squash
- 'Tom Thumb' popcorn

Focus on Foliage

1. **Annual: Flowering maple**
   Abutilon 'Souvenir de Bonn'

2. **Perennial: Blue cardinal flower**
   Lobelia siphilitica 'Blue Selection'
   ZONES: 4–8

3. **Vegetable: Red cabbage**
   Brassica oleracea cv.
   ANNUAL

4. **Herb: Silver-edged thyme**
   Thymus x citriodorus 'Argenteus'
   ZONES: 6–9

5. **Perennial: Golden elder**
   Sambucus racemosa 'Sutherland Gold'
   ZONES: 3–7

An old tin breadbox comes to life as a container for pots of bergenia and Japanese andromeda. The basket in back is filled with a pot of 'Jan Reus' tulips.

A Display for Spring

BY DENNIS SCHRADER

S PRING DOESN'T SUDDENLY BURST INTO BLOOM JUST because the calendar says it's March. In the North, winter can linger for weeks, while in the South the jump from winter into spring can happen in late January. No matter where you garden, planting up containers that herald the new season is fun and easy if you know what plants to use.

When selecting plants for my early-spring containers, I'm more discriminating than I am at other times of the year. Likely candidates include the obvious pansies and spring-flowering bulbs, but annuals, perennials, and even small shrubs and trees can be used effectively as well.

Bulbs

In autumn, when I'm planting spring-flowering bulbs in my garden beds, I often plant some in pots, too, with my spring containers in mind. I sink the newly potted bulbs into an open, unplanted area in the garden or place them in a cold frame for the winter. Not all spring-flowering bulbs lend themselves to pot culture, though. When it comes to tulips, the single and double, early and midseason Triumph groups of tulips work the best. Tall Darwin hybrids and late-flowering types are better off planted in the garden.

I've had good luck with most types of daffodils, crocuses, hyacinths, grape hyacinths, and dwarf irises. With the exception of the tulips, most of these pot-grown bulbs can be replanted in the garden, where they will continue to bloom in subsequent years. I recommend keeping the bulbs in their pots until the foliage dies back naturally, then planting the bulbs at their proper depth in the ground, adding bulb fertilizer or bone meal to each hole.

Annuals and tender perennials

The ones that can handle some frost perform well in spring containers. These long-blooming plants come in a variety of shapes, sizes, and colors and combine easily with other plants to enhance container combinations. With proper feeding and deadheading, some plants, like Marguerite and African daisies, will continue blooming into fall. When the hot weather strikes, the osteospermums put on vegetative growth and then set new buds for autumn blooms.

Perennials

When I pot up early spring–blooming perennials, like primroses, hellebores, and Virginia bluebells, I like to give them a prominent location so they can show off their stuff.

When these plants have finished blooming, they can be replanted in the garden to be enjoyed for years to come. Sometimes I group a few pots of perennials together in a larger container and camouflage the pots with some woodchip mulch. This setup demands more attention when watering but creates an instant display.

Shrubs and trees

Very often when I'm walking through a nursery in early spring I spot a shrub or small tree that is too beautiful to pass up. I buy it on impulse without a thought to where I'm going to plant it. While waiting for that perfect location to open up, I incorporate the plant into an early-spring container grouping. This way, I postpone any hasty planting scheme, and I

Shrubs, like the flowering Japanese andromeda 'Dorothy Wyckoff' in the center, make compatible container companions with annuals, perennials, and bulbs.

In fall, plant spring-flowering bulbs, like tulips, in pots as well as in the ground.

can enjoy my new purchase every time I go in or out of the house. Plants like witch hazels, forsythias, camellias, and many early-blooming rhododendrons and azaleas are candidates for spring containers. The newly emerging foliage of Japanese maples and other young deciduous trees and shrubs can also be an incredible sight, worthy of being viewed up close.

After a long, cold winter, there's nothing like the new growth of early-spring bulbs, pansies, perennials, shrubs, and even trees mixed with the earthy aroma of damp soil to refresh and invigorate my soul. All of the colors, scents, and textures arranged artfully and with a bit of whimsy contribute to a cheerful transition into spring.

In early spring, brighten up your garden with containers of cold-tolerant plants like 'Apricot Beauty' tulips, grape hyacinths, and 'Delta Lavender Blue Shades' pansies.

Chill Lovers

THE FOLLOWING PLANTS tolerate the cool temperatures of late winter and early spring in the author's Zone 7 garden on Long Island in New York.

BULBS

Crocus
Crocus spp. and cvs.
ZONES: 3–8

Daffodil
Narcissus spp. and cvs.
ZONES: 3–9

Dwarf iris
Iris reticulata and cvs.
ZONES: 5–8

Grape hyacinth
Muscari spp. and cvs.
ZONES: 3–10

Hyacinth
Hyacinthus orientalis cvs.
ZONES: 5–9

Ranunculus
Ranunculus spp. and cvs.
ZONES: 4–9

Tulip
Tulipa spp. and cvs.
ZONES: 4–8

PERENNIALS

Adonis
Adonis spp. and cvs.
ZONES: 4–9

Barrenwort
Epimedium spp. and cvs.
ZONES: 4–9

Bergenia
Bergenia spp. and cvs.
ZONES: 3–8

Corydalis
Corydalis spp. and cvs.
ZONES: 5–8

English daisy
Bellis perennis and cvs.
ZONES: 4–8

Hellebore
Helleborus spp. and cvs.
ZONES: 4–9

Pansy
Viola wittrockiana cvs.
ZONES: 4–8

Primrose
Primula spp. and cvs.
ZONES: 3–8

Virginia bluebell
Mertensia virginica
ZONES: 3–7

ANNUALS

African daisy
Arctotis spp. and cvs.

Marguerite daisy
Argyranthemum spp. and cvs.

Nemesia
Nemesia spp. and cvs.

Osteospermum
Osteospermum spp. and cvs.

Twinspur
Diascia spp.and cvs.

SHRUBS AND TREES

Azalea and rhododendron
Rhododendron spp. and cvs.
ZONES: 4–9

Camellia
Camellia japonica cvs.
ZONES: 7–8

Deutzia
Deutzia spp. and cvs.
ZONES: 5–8

Forsythia
Forsythia spp. and cvs.
ZONES: 4–9

Japanese andromeda
Pieris japonica cvs.
ZONES: 6–8

Magnolia
Magnolia spp. and cvs.
ZONES: 3–9

Winter hazel
Corylopsis spp. and cvs.
ZONES: 5–9

Winter jasmine
Jasminum nudiflorum
ZONES: 6–9

Witch hazel
Hamamelis spp. and cvs.
ZONES: 5–9

Play with contrasting colors. Dark purple alternanthera foliage serves as a foil for three bright-leaved coleus cultivars.

Sizzling Leaves for Summer Pots

BY DENNIS SCHRADER

WHEN I PICTURE THE TROPICS, I THINK OF green rain forests dotted with splashes of bright color. The vibrant, sometimes fluorescent blooms and fruits of these rain-forest plants may be the essence of the jungle landscape, but don't discount the exotics that boast colorful leaves. Plants that flaunt exciting foliage can be used to bring the lush feeling of a Caribbean island to your garden. Moreover, by planting these hot-colored plants in containers, you can go a little wild without making permanent changes to your garden.

Plants for height and focus

Zesty foliage color is easy to use because the plants don't need to be in continuous bloom to make an exciting, long-lasting arrangement. In some cases, untamed color combinations occur on the same plant, even on the same leaf. Instead of using those tired old *Dracaena* spikes to add height to a container planting, try a showy, bold-leaved *Canna* cultivar, such as 'Pretoria' (Zones 8–11), with its eye-catching green-and-gold variegation, or 'Tropicanna' (also sold as 'Phaison', Zones 8–11), which has vividly striped leaves in bright orange, red, and glowing yellow, all on a dark purple background. With that many colors on one leaf, it's easy to find other plants to accompany it.

For a slightly toned-down look on a smaller-growing plant (30 to 36 inches tall), try *Canna* 'Pink Sunburst' (Zones 8–11). Its foliage is multicolored with muted shades of olive, gold, red, violet, and rose. The entire leaf has a glossy sheen. The plant is then topped off with large, watermelon-pink blossoms in late summer.

Flaxes (*Phormium* spp. and cvs., Zones 9–10), a genus of plants that hails from New Zealand, have colorful foliage that can also provide height to mixed containers. The genus contains two species—mountain flax (*P. cookianum*, spp. *P. colensoi*) and New Zealand flax (*P. tenax*)—which have spawned many cultivars with colorful leaves.

LEFT: Flaxes like *Phormium* 'Pink Stripe' add subdued color while lending height to an arrangement.

BELOW: Vivid foliage gives a pot long-lasting drama. Hot-colored *Canna* 'Tropicanna' and purple-and-red-leaved *Phormium* 'Guardsman' take center stage in this planting.

Depending on the species or cultivar, a flax's sword-shaped leaves can grow anywhere from 18 inches to 6 feet long (photo left). They range in color from matte gray-green (*P. tenax*) to vivid stripes of yellow (*P.* 'Yellow Wave'), bronze with cream and pink (*P.* 'Sundowner'), burgundy-purple (*P. tenax* 'Atropurpureum'), and apricot (*P.* 'Apricot Queen').

Other colorful foliage plants that can be used for height are purple fountain grasses (*Pennisetum setaceum* 'Rubrum', Zones 8–11, and *P. alopecuroides* 'Burgundy Giant', Zones 6–9). These quick-growing, tender grasses add a punch of color and movement to containers. Their wispy good looks and deep plum-red color are two attributes that combine easily with almost any other plant. In full sun, 'Rubrum' will grow to a height of 3 to 3½ feet and have fuzzy, burgundy inflorescences all summer long. 'Burgundy Giant' looks more like a cornstalk and grows to a height of 6 feet. When it's grown as a container plant, it needs a substantial pot.

Fillers for the middle

Though it's a challenge to introduce vivid color schemes in shaded locations, caladiums (*Caladium* spp. and cvs., Zones 10–11) are a wonderful solution. Their large leaves come in color combinations ranging from pure white to cream, pink, and deep red. The leaves are often splashed, spotted, or streaked with other colors. Contrasting, brightly colored veins often create an interesting network of patterns on the leaf. When matched up with the exciting colors of other tender perennials like *Impatiens walleriana* cultivars (annual), tuberous begonias (*Begonia* spp. and cvs., Zones 10–11), flowering maples (*Abutilon* spp. and cvs., Zones 8–10), and fuchsias (*Fuchsia* spp. and cvs., Zones 8–10), caladiums can transform a quiet shady area into an exhilarating, colorful spot.

Another colorful foliage plant for shade is coleus (*Solenostemon scutellarioides* cvs., Zone 11). The multicolored leaves range from gentle pastels to electrifying combinations of red, orange, yellow, and pink to almost pure black. The variety of leaf shapes ranges from broadly oval to deeply lobed and scalloped to frilly, featherlike arrangements. Coleus are indispensable since they can be used to fill in between the central height element in a planting and the trailing plants along the edge. Planted alone in a container, coleus makes a colorful statement and can be placed anywhere a bit of color is needed.

Plants soften the edge

Plants belonging to the genus *Alternanthera*, which go by the common names of calico plant and blood leaf, come in a wonderful selection of shapes and colors. They range in form from tight, compact little plants with tiny, ½-inch leaves to large, sprawling, vigorous plants that can consume an entire planter if not pinched back. These plants are best used to cascade freely over the edge of a container.

Alternanthera dentata 'Rubiginosa' (Zones 10–11) is a vigorous grower, easily sprawling to a length of 24 to 30 inches. Its glossy, deep burgundy,

Caladiums add color in the shade. The large leaves come in a range of hues.

2-inch leaves are a perfect foil for yellows and golds. Even bubblegum pink and deep violet-blue work nicely with this plant. If you want an even more outrageous combination, try using *A. dentata* 'Tricolor' (Zones 9–11). It has the same leaf shape and exuberant growth as 'Rubiginosa', but the deep burgundy leaves are splashed with magenta.

Depending on the cultivars, the small, round to threadlike leaves range in color from golden yellow ('Yellow Wide Leaf') to deep blood red ('Red Fine Leaf') to rust splashed with green and yellow ('Krinkle').

The endless number of tropical combinations makes it easy to bring an exotic flair to your garden. Since container gardens last only one season, why not be daring? You may even be inspired to reproduce a delightful design in your perennial border.

Mums play a support-
ing role in this vibrant
fall border.

Containers That Last into Fall

BY DENNIS SCHRADER

THE TRANSITION FROM THE EXUBERANCE OF SUMMER, when my containers are looking their fullest and most luxuriant, to the first frost, when the more tender plants collapse, used to be an upsetting time for me. But over the last few years, I've learned that the onset of autumn doesn't have to mean the end of the container gardening season.

A trip to the garden center in September or October seems, at first glance, to yield the same old choices of mums and pansies. Although I still rely on pansies, grasses, kale, and garden mums to dress up my containers, I also use many other plants that look good into fall.

Another less expensive and more readily available source for plant material is my own garden. Taking a division from a clump of coral bells (*Heuchera* spp. and cvs.), a sedge (*Carex* spp. and cvs.), an ornamental grass, or a sedum (*Sedum* spp. and cvs.) and potting it up in summer for use in my fall containers saves quite a bit of money. Occasionally, I'll even use a plant that was part of a summer container that can withstand a frost or two, like English ivy (*Hedera helix* cvs.) or golden creeping Jenny (*Lysimachia nummularia* 'Aurea'). Other decorative materials, like cornstalks, branches, and even gourds or pumpkins can be used to round out the picture.

Repeat colors and textures

I use so many types of plants in so many pots that I've had to come up with a design strategy that works. My biggest concern is providing continuity to the design, and I do this typically by potting up a few large combination planters with an assortment of plants. Then I repeat the colors and textures I've used in the mixed planters in smaller pots with single plants and position the pots in pleasing arrangements. In general, I use crisp autumnal shades to reflect the colors of the surrounding landscape.

A fall container garden doesn't have to be elaborate to be attractive. I created a container combination using two terra-cotta pots: a tall square pot with an 18-inch opening and a shorter, round container (photo, left). I placed them along the edge of a path just off my patio, which helps draw visitors into the garden. For the taller pot, I chose muhly grass (*Muhlenbergia dumosa*) as my central plant, then added an acorus grass (*Acorus gramineus* 'Ogon'), whose bright gold-and-green-striped foliage contrasts nicely with the feathery muhly grass. I added two maroon-leaved coral bells (*Heuchera* 'Stormy Seas') and similarly shaded pansies (*Viola* x *wittrockiana* 'Antique Shades'), which work nicely with the coral bells' foliage.

A fall container doesn't have to be elaborate to be attractive.

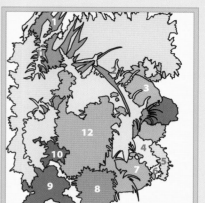

Coordinating Colors

1. *Phormium tenax* 'Atropurpureum'
2. *Salvia leucantha*
3. *Chrysanthemum* 'Luciane'
4. *Chrysanthemum* 'Valerie'
5. *Lysimachia nummularia* 'Aurea'
6. *Bergenia* 'Autumn Glory'
7. *Viola* x *wittrockiana* cvs.
8. *Euphorbia amygdaloides* 'Purpurea'
9. *Brassica oleracea* 'Redbor'
10. *Heuchera* 'Stormy Seas'
11. *Muhlenbergia dumosa*
12. *Dahlia* 'Powder Puff Mix'

For the complementary container, I didn't need another plant for height, but I did want to mimic the grass, so I chose the low-growing Mexican feather grass (*Stipa tenuissima*). Its wispy, blond, hairlike foliage softens the face of the pot behind it and, in addition, provides a good backdrop for the large, coarse, deep red leaves of flowering kale (*Brassica oleracea* 'Redbor'). These two plants make a vibrant combination when placed with a more traditional ornamental kale (*B. oleracea* 'Emperor Rose'), golden creeping Jenny (*Lysimachia nummularia* 'Aurea'), and the glowing orange blooms of pansy (*Viola* x *wittrockiana* 'Delta Orange').

Once I get the containers in place, I water them using a balanced, water-soluble fertilizer. Because the weather is cooler, the pots don't need to be watered as often as summer pots do, so I get to spend more time sitting back and enjoying the bounty that fall has to offer. And come December, if the snow and ice hold off long enough, the ornamental kale, dried grasses, and seed heads of some of the perennials from my fall containers might even make it into a few of my winter displays.

Branches and Berries

1. **Flowering dogwood**
   Cornus florida and cvs.
   ZONES: 5–8

2. **Holly**
   Ilex spp. and cvs.
   ZONES: 5–9

3. **Japanese andromeda**
   Pieris japonica cv.
   ZONES: 6–8

4. **Oriental bittersweet**
   Celastrus orbiculatus
   ZONES: 4–8

5. **Sedum**
   Sedum cv.
   ZONES: 3–9

6. **White pine**
   Pinus strobus
   ZONES: 4–9

Festive Pots for Winter

BY CYNTHIA EICHENGREEN

EVERY SUMMER, THE WINDOW BOXES AND CONTAINERS in my neighborhood overflow with brilliant flowers. And every winter, I see those same window boxes and containers sitting empty. For years, mine were no exception. As I walked out my front door each winter morning, I'd be greeted by three concrete pots full of crusted-over dirt. This was not exactly the welcome I wanted at the entrance to my home.

The creation of the first of what I call my "holiday pots" began on a frantic December morning when I was expecting company, and the containers on the front porch looked particularly barren. I ran to the backyard, cut some holly and cedar branches, and stuck them in the pots with some fake berries because my real hollies had none that year. The result was charming, so I left the arrangement until it started to turn brown and dry out, which was sometime in March. By then, it was time to plant spring flowers.

I live in Eugene, Oregon (Zone 8), where there is little freezing, so I can use any kind of pot for my winter containers, except Mexican terra-cotta, which tends to flake. People who live in colder regions (generally, Zone 6 and lower) should pay special attention to pots they use in winter, since some materials will not stand up to repeated freezing and thawing. In these areas, clay and ceramic pots should be brought inside for the winter or they may crack. For winter displays in cold areas, use wood, plastic, or concrete pots, which are not as bothered by freezes.

One trick I've learned that works in both mild and cold climates is to buy next year's spring shrubs (especially evergreens and conifers) and use them in containers over the winter. The shrubs stay green throughout the winter and give a solid performance. In the spring, I simply unpot them and move them to their permanent homes. Shrubs in containers are often quite inexpensive at the end of the season and can be tossed out in the spring if you don't want them in the garden or if the plants don't survive.

I place my winter containers in protected locations in my garden where they can take advantage of a microclimate that is a little warmer than the rest of the garden. I have window boxes nestled against the house and pots placed on the south-facing side of my house or tucked among trees and shrubs. The additional bit of protection the containers receive from these locations makes a big difference in the performance of the plants.

Generally, my winter containers need less water than my summer ones do. In cold climates, the winter containers don't need any water because they will freeze solid, but in milder climates, they need to be watered occasionally unless there is regular rainfall. Window boxes, especially, need to be monitored for water because they are usually located under the eaves where rainfall may not reach them. Fortunately, I've found that florist's cyclamen (*Cyclamen persicum* cvs., particularly the dwarf fragrant strains) prefer dry, cool soil. Since these plants will continue to bloom throughout my mild winter as long as they don't

Branches and Berries for Pots

Variegated holly

Winterberry holly

Berries

Beautyberry
Callicarpa spp. and cvs.

Euonymus
Euonymus spp. and cvs.

Holly
Ilex spp. and cvs.

Winterberry holly
Ilex verticillata

Yew
Taxus spp. and cvs.

Redtwig dogwood

Blue spruce

Branches

Firethorn
Pyracantha spp. and cvs.

Fir
Abies spp. and cvs.

Osmanthus
Osmanthus spp. and cvs.

Pine
Pinus spp. and cvs.

Redtwig dogwood
Cornus alba and cvs.

Spruce
Picea spp. and cvs.

get too wet, I use them in my window boxes and water them infrequently.

For containers in which I'm not growing plants, I select branches and compose an arrangement. I've seen pinecones and even Christmas lights strung through window boxes for added interest. Where winters are especially cold and brutal, the greens may have to be replaced periodically.

Every year, I experiment with different greens. Short sprigs of pine tips look like clumps of fescue when they are tucked in a pot, and branches of weeping conifers positioned to drape over the edge of a container can be especially graceful. I have even used a few cut flowers from the florist on hospitable days. The flowers, of course, last only a day or two, but they make quite an impact, particularly when company is coming. During the dark days of winter, a cheerful pot near the door lifts my spirits and welcomes those who come to visit.

TOP: This box has weeping pine, spruce, fir, redtwig dogwood, mountain laurel, winterberry holly, and a string of lights. It gives people something to look at from inside as well as out.

RIGHT: Evergreens and conifers make perfect winter pot plants. With artificial berries tucked in the pots will look great into early spring.

The fine textures of these plants are united by soothing green hues.

Trees in Pots

BY FINE GARDENING EDITORS

I MAGINE YOURSELF AT THE END OF YOUR WORKDAY SITTING in a beautiful garden sipping a cup of tea, relaxing, and reflecting on the beauty of your surroundings. A group of graceful trees brings nature up close, cools the air, and whispers the secrets of the breeze in your ear. The scent of damp earth and flowers is close at hand. Though we are not all blessed with a country home to indulge this fantasy, most of us have a patio, deck, or balcony, and, believe it or not, that's all the space needed to create a beautiful garden of small trees in containers.

Besides creating a private paradise, trees in containers are useful for other reasons. When you use them near the house, they blur the line between inside and outside, guide guests to the door, or entice you outside to enjoy the day. They can also serve as focal points, drawing your attention to a certain part of the garden. Or they can be used as a screen along the edge of a driveway or patio.

Trees in containers also lend versatility to a patio or garden because they can be moved around. A flowering tree can be brought up close in spring and summer, replaced by a tree with great fall color, then succeeded by an evergreen to complete the year. It does take more gardening expertise to grow trees in containers, but the reward makes the effort worthwhile. Regular attention to watering and root-pruning is really all it takes to have a healthy tree in a pot.

Dwarf or small trees are best suited to container culture

There are many exquisite trees that can be used for patio containers, but the first criterion should be to choose a plant with characteristics you love. Do you love bright colors or long for cooling greens? Do bold statements excite you or do you prefer delicate features? Do you want a slender, upright look or lust after a weeping or cascading tree?

ABOVE LEFT: The red xoropetalum complements the brick walkway.

ABOVE RIGHT: The feet of this snow bush tree are covered by coleus and Japanese forest grass

On a more practical level, choose a tree that is naturally small at maturity, is in excellent health, is at least one zone hardier than yours, and has been container grown all its life. Dwarf Japanese maples (*Acer palmatum* cvs., Zones 6–8) and dwarf Canadian hemlocks (*Tsuga canadensis* cvs., Zones 4–8) are among my favorites, and both do well in the partial shade most of us prefer for our outdoor seating areas. Trees require a regular pruning and repotting regimen, so the more slowly the tree grows, the less often you will have to repot it.

When choosing a container, consider that the tree will most likely stay outside all year. If you wish to use a ceramic or terra-cotta container, be sure it is high-fired or it will crack when it freezes. I like to use containers that are wider than they are tall because they are far more stable, and I enjoy planting ground covers and dwarf bulbs as underplantings.

Plant a small tree in a container just larger than its roots, then each year move it up to the next-size-larger pot until you reach the largest pot size you'd like to have. As a general rule, a 15-gallon pot will comfortably hold a 4- to 5-foot-tall tree and a 30-gallon pot will support an 8-foot-tall tree. Casters on the bottom of large pots will simplify moving them around.

Use a sand-based soil and just a little fertilizer

The soil used in container growing is very important and serves two main functions: It supports and anchors the tree, and it provides a medium for the delivery of nutrients, moisture, and air. Different plants have different requirements, but in general, container-grown trees prefer a sand-based soil. Sandy soils help develop the fine, fibrous roots necessary to sustain the trees in their pots, and sand is dense, so it adds weight and stability to the container. Peat moss or ground bark should be included to hold air and moisture, and good compost can be added to provide nutrients. The proportion I use for most trees is 1 part coarse sand to 3 parts ground bark to 1 part compost. The purchase of a good, commercially available potting mix with similar ingredients simplifies the process and is sure to get you off to a good start.

Since the soil is free-draining, you will need to water trees in containers more often than those in the ground. Check the moisture level of the soil several inches below the surface and when it is feeling dry, thoroughly water the container. You will need to water more often if you site your tree in full sun in a hot climate. In the heat of the summer in my gardens in California, I often water three times a week.

Fertilizer requirements vary, but in general, a little goes a long way. With trees in containers, you are not trying to encourage rapid growth. You want your trees to be healthy and happy, but the goal is slow growth. Avoid fertilizing with too much nitrogen. Many people find fish emulsion to be the perfect fertilizer. It is a complete food, is low in nitrogen, and is easy to use. It should be applied sparingly but regularly during the growing season. I don't recommend slow-release fertilizer because it tends to cause leaf-margin burn.

For long-term health, be sure to root-prune

It is essential to root-prune a containerized tree during late-winter dormancy every two to five years. Only the newest root tips are able to absorb water and nutrients, and root-pruning stimulates the growth of these tips. Root-pruning is not difficult. Remove all circling roots

TIP

Turning Large Containers

It can be cumbersome, if not impossible, to turn large potted plants in order to ensure even sun exposure, remove spent blooms, cut flowers, inspect for insects, check the soil condition, and so forth. Even wheeled plant stands can be difficult to make work since they hold water and don't always suit the pot for which they were intended. A better approach is to fill a saucer, just a bit larger than the base of the pot, with florists' marbles and set the pot on top of them. The pot will have drainage and turn easily, and the marbles never deteriorate. If, at the end of the season, the marbles are covered in sediment, a soak in a vinegar solution before reusing them will clean them up.

and cut away an eighth to a quarter of the root ball from the bottom using your pruning shears or a garden knife. (If a root ball is severely overgrown, you may have to use a saw to remove the bottom 2 or 3 inches.) Then use a serrated knife to make four to six vertical 2- to 3-inch wedge cuts that extend into the sides a couple of inches. Replant the tree with fresh soil, filling in the gaps around the edge of the pot.

Most trees you choose for a container won't require above-ground pruning except for the regular maintenance of removing dead, diseased, or damaged branches. You should always prune in late winter, during dormancy, before the buds break in the spring. If you wish to shape your tree or thin it out to show off some interesting bark, think carefully before you cut, since you can't put it back once you've taken it off.

This combination, which mixes eye-catching foliage with color flowers, looks beautiful from inside the house.

Creative Ways to Design a Window Box

BY GARY R. KEIM

THERE COMES A TIME WHEN A GARDEN NEEDS A jolt of novelty or a finishing touch to bring it together. One way to do this is to add window boxes to your home. These details fuse indoors and out and make the house and garden whole. I have them adorning the facade of my home, where they add charm to the Cape Cod–style architecture. One of my favorite aspects of gardening beneath the windowsills is that I can see the colorful plants from inside my house. I've even gone so far as to tie the colors of the plants into the color schemes of my rooms.

But why stop at the front of your home? Window boxes are also ideal for the side and back of the house as well as deck rails, walls, balustrades, and broad, wide steps. I think "flower boxes" is a more appropriate name for these versatile containers because they aren't just for windows. I use flower boxes to dress up a solitary window at the back of my house. I also use them on the railings of my deck to add to the color and variety of my other containers without taking up valuable floor space.

Wherever your flower boxes are located, you won't truly enjoy them unless they look good. The concepts of container design apply here, too: a mix of plants that are tall, bulky, or cascading. Here are four strategies to help you get the most from your boxes.

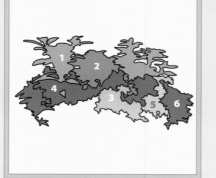

A Living Wall

1. Persian shield
Strobilanthes dyerianus
ZONES: 9–11

2. 'Haines' coleus
Solenostemon scutellarioides
'Haines'
ANNUAL

3. Fusion™ Heat impatiens
Impatiens
Fusion Heat
ANNUAL

4. Babywing® Pink begonia
Begonia
Babywing Pink
ANNUAL

5. Diamond Frost® spurge
Euphorbia
Diamond Frost
ANNUAL

6. Sweet Caroline® Purple sweet potato vine
Ipomoea batatas
Sweet Caroline Purple
ZONE: 11

Turn a railing into a living wall

This flower box hanging from a deck railing is a border unto itself. The height of this composition adds privacy to the deck by screening the adjacent drive-way and the neighbor's house. Two tall, elegant Persian shields do most of the work, surrounding a 'Haines' coleus that complements in leaf shape and color. The coleus also adds a bright punch to the container, echoed by the impatiens covering the coleus's feet. Babywing begonias and a Diamond Frost spurge fill in around the legs of the tall plants without overwhelming the container. Sweet Caroline Purple sweet potato vine cascades from the box, connecting the purple of the Persian shields to the sur-rounding containers.

Repeat plant variety
in paired boxes

If your house has a pair of windows on either side of the front door repetition is crucial for a cohesive design. Making each box an exact duplicate of the other can be boring. To add more visual interest, consider planting each box to be a mirror image of the other.

Being in such a highly visible spot, these boxes need to work with the house. The orange and yellow leaves of 'Freckles' coleus contrast with plum-colored shutters and add height to the design. The flowers of the Fusion™ Glow impatiens pick up on this theme, too. The chartreuse foliage of the sweet potato vine gives more light to this combination, and its cascading stems, along with the wishbone flower, soften the edge of the box, connecting it to the ground and the house to the garden.

Repeating Plants

1. **'Freckles' coleus**
   Solenostemon scutellarioides 'Freckles'
   ANNUAL

2. **Fusion Glow impatiens**
   Impatiens Fusion Glow
   ANNUAL

3. **Catalina® Blue wishbone flower**
   Torenia Catalina Blue
   ANNUAL

4. **Sweet Caroline® Light Green sweet potato vine**
   Ipomoea batatas Sweet Caroline Light Green
   ZONE: 11

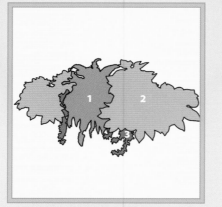

A Shady Box Shines

1. 'Kimberly Queen' Australian sword fern
Nephrolepis obliterata 'Kimberly Queen'
TROPICAL

2. 'Lifelime' coleus
Solenostemon scutellarioides 'Lifelime'
ANNUAL

3. Variegated English ivy
Hedera helix cv.
ZONES: 5–11

Make a shady box shine

This predominantly green planting is a study in contrasting leaf shapes and textures. Attached to a lone window that looks from a kitchen out to the deck, it receives no direct sunlight. In the center, an Australian sword fern anchors the planting with its height and mass. The foliage of 'Lifelime' coleus contrasts wonderfully with the shape and texture of the fern but complements its color. The coleus should be trimmed periodically to make them bushy and to keep them from overwhelming the fern. A variegated ivy dangles from beneath the fern and coleus, softening and hiding the box in the same manner that a curtain graces a window.

Eye-catching plants grab attention

Flower boxes need to pack a punch if they are going to grab attention from the street. Forgo many of the plants normally used in boxes for something more eye-catching. In this box, the elephant's ear and the begonia immediately grab your interest. The elephant's ear has huge, exotic leaves, but the begonia has the center spot and bright red blooms. Both plants have enough connecting them (pointed, glossy leaves, for example) so that the composition isn't disrupted. The foliage of the caladium in the rear of the box strengthens the connection between the two stars by echoing the shape of the elephant's ear and the color of the begonia's flowers.

Eye-Catching Plants

1. **'Polly' elephant's ear**
   Alocasia x *amazonica* 'Polly'
   ZONES: 10–11

2. **Dragon Wing® Pink begonia**
   Begonia Dragon Wing Pink
   ANNUAL

3. **Caladium**
   Caladium cv.
   TROPICAL

4. **Golden creeping Jenny**
   Lysimachia nummularia 'Aurea'
   ZONES: 4–8

5. **'Amethyst' wishbone flower**
   Torenia 'Amethyst'
   ANNUAL

TIP

Add Height to a Window Box

Here's an easy way to add vertical height to a window box so you can enjoy your plantings from inside your home. Push a 5-foot-long willow branch into each end of your planter, gently bend it into an arch, and secure it at the top. Plant scarlet runner beans or morning glories at the base of the willow branches, along with a few complementary plants to fill in the box. The result will be spectacular.

Exciting compositions spring from unusual combinations. The author used tall, spiky cattail (*Typha laxmannii*), broad-leaved cranberry taro (*Colocasia rubra*), and a floating clump of variegated spider lily (*Hymenocallis caribaea* 'Variegata') to create a dynamic design.

Design a Simple Water Garden

BY JOE TOMOCIK

I'M INTO LITTLE WATER GARDENS IN A BIG WAY. I'VE found my greatest challenges—and my greatest delights—in designing water gardens for small containers. Small-container water gardens are actually a collection of submerged potted plants, so redesigning a planting is as simple as moving the pots around. And the plants are tough—most are almost hard to kill and require virtually no maintenance. All you need is a sunny spot with at least six hours of direct sun a day, something that holds water, and a few plants. For me, small-container water gardens have been an endless source of inspiration. And once you've mastered a small container, think of what you can do in a big water garden.

Half barrels are perfect choices

The first step in designing a small water garden is deciding on the container. Anything that holds water qualifies. Even if it doesn't, there's still hope—holes can usually be plugged with inexpensive corks to make a container watertight. I find widely sold half barrels to be perfect. At 24 inches wide by 16 inches deep, they are ideally sized to accommodate a dramatic display. The problem, though, is that toxins oozing from the wood can foul both water and plants. My solution is to purchase a durable, plastic liner made to fit perfectly. These liners are available at many garden centers. Or you could line the barrel with a flexible PVC liner; just be sure to use at least two layers if the material is less than 10 mil thick; otherwise, the liner will only last a year or two.

I've also used clay and plastic containers. To keep water from seeping into and through the porous clay of a ceramic container, I apply two coats of sealer. I also enjoy using black plastic containers that look like cast-iron pots. I've found them available in three sizes—15, 12, and 9 inches across—and sometimes I like to display them all as a group.

Use plants that contrast

Water, cupped in a container or basin, is a thing of beauty. Its flickering reflections are a welcome presence in any garden. But dressing it up with plants transports the display to a whole new dimension. I like to create compositions that are vibrant and dynamic, so I use plants with contrasting shapes, colors, and sizes. For me, the more contrast, the better.

I like to combine the tall, slender, spiky shapes of an erect, fine-leaved marginal plant like yellow flag iris (*Iris pseudacorus*, Zones 5–8) or sweet flag (*Acorus calamus*, Zones 4–11) with the broad-leaved foliage of an easy-to-grow tropical marginal like taro (*Colocasia* spp. and cvs., Zones 9–11)—especially one of the varieties with variegated or dark purple leaves. Marginal plants are those that are usually placed along the edges of a water garden; in the wild, they grow in shallow water.

For a special touch, I might add a variegated spider lily (*Hymenocallis caribaea* 'Variegata', Zone 11, photo, p. 106) or a clump of brightly colored chameleon plant (*Houttuynia cordata* 'Chameleon', Zones 6–11). I especially like using plants that have a story of their own: Pitcher plants (*Sarracenia* spp. and cvs., Zones 2–11), for example, eat insects, digesting small bugs in the recesses of their large, trumpet-shaped leaves.

To finish off a planting, I sprinkle a few small floating plants—like water lettuce (*Pistia stratiotes*, Zone 11) or water hyacinth (*Eichhornia crassipes*, Zones 10–11)—over the surface of the water.

I also might soften the hard edge of the container by letting a cascading plant like water mint (*Mentha aquatica*, Zones 6–9), with its fragrant foliage and powder blue flowers, tumble over the side.

Whatever plants I use, I try to keep them in scale with the container. There are no strict guidelines to follow, so I just aim for a plant-and-container combination that looks harmonious and proportionate.

How to Create an Arrangement

UNLESS THE CONTAINER IS TO BE DISPLAYED in the round, place a tall, spiky plant at the center rear to create a dramatic backdrop. Then use a broad-leaved plant (or two) in front or to one side, where its generously sized leaves will contrast sharply with the whiplike fronds of taller plants. Use pavers or upside-down empty pots to vary the height of plants. Plants in containers of varied sizes will need to be positioned individually in a small water garden.

Use pavers and empty pots to vary the height of plants.

A water garden can be as simple as a pot full of water lettuce (*Pistia stratiotes*).

Regardless of the number of plants you use, how and where you place plants in the container is of paramount importance. The plants should fit as a unit to create the picture you want. First, determine how the planting will be viewed. Designing a container that will be seen from one or two directions is a lot easier than making one that's meant to be viewed from all sides.

For either kind of design, I arrange and rearrange the plants until I get the effect I'm looking for. It's easy to change the height and position of plants by perching them on bricks or empty, overturned containers. Most marginals, whether their leaves are thin and vertical or broad and horizontal, give excellent results when their crowns are placed no deeper than 6 inches beneath the water's surface. Only after the main parts have been positioned do I begin to add accents like floating or cascading plants or, for a special touch, an eye-catching specimen.

Container care is easy

Once your water garden has been planted, caring for it is simple. If the plants don't seem to be thriving, more than likely the problem is not enough light. If that's the case, then move the container to a brighter spot. If it's too heavy to lift, remove the plants, empty out the water, move the container, and then rearrange it.

Water plants grow quickly, but even so, I encourage them by using fertilizer tablets. For new plants, I delay fertilizing until they show signs of growth. When a plant gets big, I divide and repot it in heavy clay soil. Dense soils won't cloud the water when containers are moved, and just to be sure, I always firm the soil fairly tightly before lowering the con-

Use only a few plants

The first mistake beginning water gardeners make is jamming too many plants into their container. Though a half barrel–size container easily accommodates up to four plants in 2-gallon pots and a host of floating plants, there's no need to use that many. An overcrowded container often results in designs that are chaotic. Keep it simple. Especially when you are starting, it's easiest to make pleasing designs with only two or three plants. As you gain experience, you can graduate to more complicated compositions using greater numbers and varieties of plants.

Placement is important.
Plants and pots should fit
together as a unit to create
an eye-catching effect.

Great Plants for a Container Water Garden

DESIGNING SUCCESSFUL CONTAINER WATER GARDENS is a matter of knowing which aquatic plants to use. The following list of plants has worked well for me. Some of these aquatic plants can be invasive, however, and should be used only in containers—not in ponds.

Fantastic floaters

Floating moss
Salvinia rotundifolia
ZONES: 10–11

This minute but exquisite floater has ¾-inch-long leaves and is ideal for small container water gardens.

Water hyacinth
Eichhornia crassipes
ZONES: 10–11

Characterized by its swollen, balloonlike leaves, this floater has lilac-blue, irislike flowers that bloom about 6 inches above the water's surface.

Water lettuce
Pistia stratiotes
ZONES: 11

This palm-size plant has soft, wrinkled, light green leaves with a velvety texture. It tolerates more shade than many aquatic plants.

Cascading plants

Parrot feather
Myriophyllum aquaticum
ZONES: 9–11

As the common name suggests, this is a plant with soft, feathery tufts of foliage.

Water mint
Mentha aquatica
ZONES: 6–9

This fast-growing plant has fuzzy, roundish leaves that may be reddish purple in full sun. Its foliage is fragrant when crushed. The plant bears a profusion of tiny, powder blue flowers.

Plants with vertical foliage

Dwarf cattail
Typha laxmannii
ZONES: 4–10

This species has graceful, 4-foot spires of foliage topped, in late summer, by easily recognized brown flowers that look like sausage links. A dwarf variety, *T. minima* 'Europa', is well suited to small containers.

Dwarf papyrus
Cyperus haspans
ZONES: 9–10

This plant has bell-shaped flower clusters atop slightly drooping, 18- to 24-inch stems.

Prairie cordgrass
Spartina pectinata
ZONES: 4–7

The rugged, grassy foliage grows to about 5 feet tall. It sways in the breeze and turns golden brown in late summer.

Sweet flag
Acorus calamus
ZONES: 4–11

The irislike foliage of this grassy plant grows 2 to 4 feet tall and, when broken, releases an invigorating, fruity fragrance.

Broad-leaved plants

Calla lily
Zantedeschia aethiopica
and cvs.
ZONES: 8–10

This plant has arrowhead-shaped leaves and lovely flowers—actually, they're spathes—available in a rainbow of pastel hues. It grows to 2 feet tall.

Canna
Canna cvs.
ZONES: 8–11

These big-leaved tropicals are available in foliage colors ranging from deep green to purple and pink, with some varieties, especially *C.* 'Pretoria', displaying a striking, striped variegation. Heights range from 2 or 3 feet to about 6 feet. Flowers bloom in shades of red, yellow, pink, or orange.

Duck potato
Sagittaria latifolia
ZONES: 5–11

This easily grown American native has three-petaled, white flowers and impressive arrowhead-shaped leaves. It grows up to 4 feet tall.

Taro
Colocasia esculenta and cvs.
ZONES: 9–11

Excellent water-garden plants with huge leaves that contrast dramatically with slender-foliaged, upright plants. Some varieties have deep burgundy-colored or variegated leaves. It grows to about 3½ feet tall.

Marginals that dress up a water garden

Chameleon plant
Houttuynia cordata
'Chameleon'
ZONES: 6–11

This fast-spreading plant forms a delightful, distinctive mound of red-, green-, and cream-variegated foliage. It belongs at the front of any display.

Variegated spider lily
Hymenocallis caribaea
'Variegata'
ZONE: 11

This one will make eyes pop with its electric, variegated, green-and-white leaves. It also produces exotic, fragrant, white blooms.

Yellow pitcher plant
Sarracenia flava
ZONES: 7–10

This curiosity has erect, trumpet-shaped, insect-eating leaves, which are deeply veined with whites and reds. It will reach up to 30 inches in height.

Taro

Yellow pitcher plant

Chameleon plant

Water lily

Water hyacinth

tainer back into the water. If the plants seem too robust, I limit their growth by keeping them in small pots and trimming off the oldest and tallest leaves.

There's no need to change the water in a container garden, although you should top it off every few days to replace liquid that may have evaporated. I've never had problems with mosquitoes breeding in containers, but if you want to eliminate any chance of establishing a breeding ground for insects, you might wash the larvae out by overfilling your container with water or add a few mosquito fish (*Gambusia affinis*), voracious eaters that feed on mosquito larvae. Aquatic nurseries have also developed specially formulated products for killing mosquito larvae and *Bacillus thuringiensis* (bt) dunks are also effective at controlling mosquitoes.

When winter comes, it doesn't have to mean the end of the garden. Most water plants can be brought indoors and used as houseplants or even placed in a tub of water in a cool basement. Hardy plants could be left in the container but may need protection against freezing. Where winters are severe, birdbath-type heaters can prevent your container water garden from turning into a giant ice cube.

When spring comes, plants are ready to divide. Use the extras to start a new water garden. By then, you'll be immersed in the world of aquatic plants.

SOURCES

The following mail-order nurseries offer the widest selection of the aquatic plants featured.

- Maryland Aquatic Nurseries; 410-557-7615; www.marylandaquatic.com

- Windy Oaks Aquatics; 262-594-3033; www.windyoaksaquatics.com

Because most of these plants are from the yellow family the red coleus is all the more vibrant.

A Gallery of Successful Designs

BY FINE GARDENING EDITORS

I N THE OLD DAYS, WHEN A GLIMPSE OF A STOCKING WAS
looked on as something shocking, the choices for container plants
amounted to geraniums, petunias, and ivy. Today, there's a ban-
quet out there. Even the golden oldies are turning up in dashing
new colors, sizes, shapes, and forms. So if you're attracted to container
gardening but unsure of what to do, dive right in, relying on tried-and-
true varieties or experimenting with new specimens.

The design examples on the following pages will provide boundless
inspiration. Keep in mind a few things: In terms of plant material, your
only real limitation is budget; pots and nontraditional vessels are available in myriad shapes, sizes, and colors, and can provide just as much
drama as the plants themselves (see pages 215–229 for some great
container options). Most of all, have fun. Containers can add pizzazz
to even the most ordinary of landscapes.

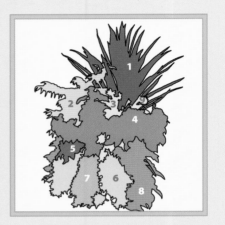

A Thrilling Combination

1. **Cordyline**
   Cordyline australis
   'Red Sensation'
   ZONES: 10–11

2. **Tiger eyes sumac**
   Rhus typhina
   'Bailtiger'
   ZONES: 3–8

3. **Black-eyed Susan**
   Rudbeckia hirta
   'Prairie Sun'
   ZONES: 3–7

4. **Coleus**
   Solenostemon scutellarioides
   'Sedona'
   ZONE: 11

5. **Heuchera**
   Heuchera 'Obsidian'
   ZONES: 3–8

6. **Creeping zinnia**
   Sanvitalia procumbens 'Sunbini'
   ANNUAL

7. **Golden creeping Jenny**
   Lysimachia nummularia
   'Goldilocks'
   ZONES: 4–8

8. **Sweet potato vine**
   Ipomoea batatas
   'Margarita'
   ZONE: 11

9. **Zinnia**
   Zinnia elegans
   'Dreamland Yellow'
   ANNUAL

CONDITIONS: Full sun

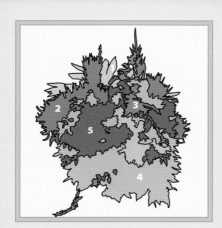

Fantastic Foliage

1. **Shell ginger**
   Alpinia zerumbet
   'Variegata'
   ZONES: 14–15

2. **Ribbon bush**
   *Homalocladium
   platycladum*
   ZONE: 11

3. **Golden jasmine**
   Jasminum officinale
   'Aureum'
   ZONES: 9–10

4. **Sweet potato vine**
   Ipomoea batatas
   'Margarita'
   ZONE: 11

5. **Coleus**
   *Solenostemon
   scutellarioides*
   'Trailing Black'
   ZONE: 11

CONDITIONS: Full sun to partial shade

Spectacular Succulents

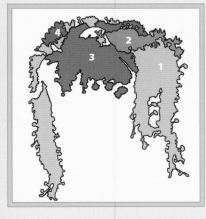

1. **Dichondra**
   Dichondra argentea
   'Silver Falls'
   ANNUAL

2. **Echeveria**
   Echeveria 'Afterglow'
   ZONES: 9–11

3. **Hens and chicks**
   Sempervivum spp.
   and cvs.
   ZONES: 4–11

4. **Thick plant**
   Pachyphytum
   compactum
   ZONES: 12–15

CONDITIONS: Full sun

A Splash of Red

1. **Phormium**
   Phormium
   'Yellow Wave'
   ZONES: 8–10

2. **Black-eyed Susan**
   Rudbeckia fulgida var.
   sullivantii 'Goldsturm'
   ZONES: 4–9

3. **Evergreen veronica**
   Hebe speciosa
   'Tricolor'
   ZONES: 10–11

4. **Japanese forest grass**
   Hakonechloa macra
   'Aureola'
   ZONES: 5–9

5. **Sage**
   Salvia officinalis
   ZONES: 5–8

6. **Coleus**
   Solenostemon scutellarioides
   'Sedona'
   ZONE: 11

CONDITIONS: Full sun to partial shade

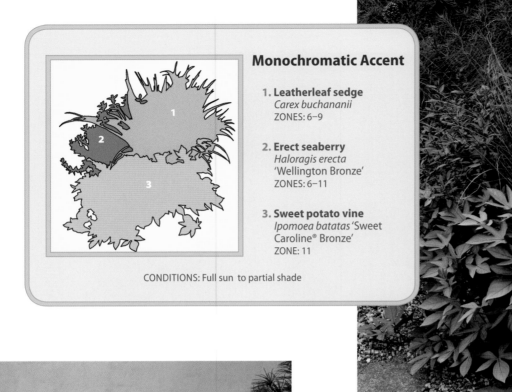

Monochromatic Accent

1. **Leatherleaf sedge**
   Carex buchananii
   ZONES: 6–9

2. **Erect seaberry**
   Haloragis erecta
   'Wellington Bronze'
   ZONES: 6–11

3. **Sweet potato vine**
   Ipomoea batatas 'Sweet
   Caroline® Bronze'
   ZONE: 11

CONDITIONS: Full sun to partial shade

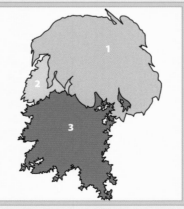

Season-long Backdrop

1. **Caladium**
   Caladium bicolor 'White
   Christmas'
   ZONE: 9–11

2. **Impatiens**
   Impatiens walleriana 'Tioga
   White'
   ANNUAL

3. **English ivy**
   Hedera helix cv.
   ZONES: 5–11

CONDITIONS: Partial shade

Tricolor Beauty

1. **'Gartenmeister Bonstedt' upright fuchsia**
   Fuchsia 'Gartenmeister Bonstedt'
   ZONES: 9–10

2. **New Wonder® scaevola**
   Scaevola aemula New Wonder
   ZONES: 10–11

3. **'Limelight' licorice plant**
   Helichrysum petiolare 'Limelight'
   ZONES: 10–11

CONDITIONS: Full sun to partial shade

Pot of Magenta

1. **Purple fountain grass**
   Pennisetum setaceum
   'Rubrum'
   ZONES: 8–11

2. **'Blackie' sweet potato
   vine**
   Ipomoea batatas
   'Blackie'
   ZONE: 11

3. **Verbena**
   Verbena hybrida cv.
   ZONES: 9–11

4. **Persian shield**
   Strobilanthes dyerianus
   ZONES: 9–11

CONDITIONS: Full sun

Packing a Punch

1. **Mandevilla**
   Mandevilla cv.
   ZONE: 11

2. **Geranium**
   Pelargonium cv.
   ZONE: 11

3. **Flowering tobacco**
   Nicotiana sanderae cv.
   ANNUAL

4. **Heliotrope**
   *Heliotropium
   arborescens* cv.
   ANNUAL

5. **Petunia**
   Petunia cv.
   ANNUAL

CONDITIONS: Full sun

Finely Textured Drama

1. **Purple fountain grass**
   Pennisetum setaceum 'Rubrum'
   ZONES: 8–11

2. **Cardoon**
   Cynara cardunculus
   ZONES: 7–10

3. **'Crystal Palace Gem' geranium**
   Pelargonium 'Crystal Palace Gem'
   ZONE: 11

4. **'Outback Sunset' dense-flowered loosestrife**
   Lysimachia congestiflora 'Outback Sunset'
   ZONES: 6–9

CONDITIONS: Full sun

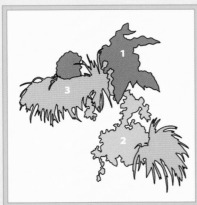

Artistic Combination

1. African mask
Alocasia amazonica
NOT HARDY BELOW ZONE 11

2. Rieger begonia
Begonia hiemalis cv.
ZONES: 10–11

3. 'Ogon' sweet flag
Acorus gramineus 'Ogon'
ZONES: 6–10

CONDITIONS: Partial to full shade

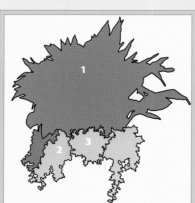

Timeless Beauty

1. **Cast-iron plant**
   Aspidistra elatior
   ZONES: 7–11

2. **English ivy**
   Hedera helix cv.
   ZONES: 5–11

3. **Diamond Frost® euphorbia**
   Euphorbia Diamond Frost®
   ZONES: 10–11

CONDITIONS: Partial to full shade

Summer Radiance

1. **'Cherries Jubilee' allamanda**
   Allamanda cathartica 'Cherries Jubilee'
   ZONES: 10–11

2. **Lantana**
   Lantana camara cv.
   ZONE: 11

3. **'Purple Lady' blood leaf**
   Iresine 'Purple Lady'
   ZONE: 11

4. **'Gold Brocade' coleus**
   Solenostemon scutellarioides 'Gold Brocade'
   ZONE: 11

5. **Creeping wire vine**
   Muehlenbeckia axillaris
   ZONES: 8–10

CONDITIONS: Full sun to partial shade

Great Plants

Planting in containers gives you the opportunity to move plants to different locations based on weather.

Plants for Year-Round Containers

BY MUFFIN EVANDER

WHEN THE AIR TURNS CHILLY IN FALL, gardeners often discard, propagate, or find a home in the ground for their outdoor potted plants. It's a pity because much of this is a waste of effort and plants. Many perennials and shrubs can live for several years in a container. By taking advantage of this characteristic, you can reduce the amount of time and money you spend on your pots. Your containers can provide you with year-round interest, depending on the plants you choose, and you can lend consistency to your designs.

For a plant, life in a container is much different than one in the ground. Containers can provide excellent drainage, but the plants depend on you for water and nutrients. Shrubs and larger perennials often stay smaller in a pot, though this depends on the plant, climate, and container. Also, containers don't insulate a plant's roots from winter temperatures.

The general rule of thumb for container-plant survival through the winter is that the plant should be hardy to two zones colder than your USDA Hardiness Zone. Here are some of the best plants that are not only tough enough to survive the cold but also look great while doing it.

Summer

'Golden Sword' Yucca

LIGHT:
Full Sun

SIZE:
2 to 3 feet tall

ZONES:
4–11

'Golden Sword' yucca combines with almost anything

I highly recommend 'Golden Sword' yucca (*Yucca filamentosa* 'Golden Sword', Zones 4–11) because it combines easily with so many plants. Its 2-inch-wide, swordlike leaves have margins that are thin and dark green, centers of golden yellow, and curly fibers along the edges. Having a spiky, architectural shape, it grows 2 to 3 feet high with equal spread. This yucca tolerates some shade but thrives in sunny, dry conditions. In summer, creamy white, fragrant flowers emerge from the center of the plant on 3- to 6-foot-tall stems. In late winter, the foliage may get a little flat, but it will perk up again in spring. Pull off the old foliage to maintain a tidy appearance.

Spring

Fall

Winter

Emerald arborvitae works where you need some height

Emerald arborvitae (*Thuja occidentalis* 'Emerald', syn. 'Smaragd', Zones 2–7) provides excellent year-round interest because it maintains its rich green color in winter. The upright, narrow habit of this cultivar of our native arborvitae fits the bill as the vertical accent that many containers need. The shape and texture of its foliage make it easy to combine with other plants. A container will keep it well under its natural size of 15 feet high and 4 feet wide. Plant it in full sun or light shade, but protect it from deer.

Bergenia has bold leaves that shine in containers

With its green, glossy, oval leaves, bergenia (*Bergenia cordifolia* and cvs., Zones 3–8) is one of my favorite plants because it is a strong grower that provides a bold element in a container design. The leaves are anywhere from 10 to 20 inches long and 6 to 8 inches wide, and turn a gorgeous burgundy in fall. Bergenia flowers in early spring on 12- to 15-inch-long stalks; the pink blossoms resemble hyacinths. The plant actually performs better in my containers than in my beds, perhaps because of the excellent drainage. Grow it in full sun or light shade.

FACING PAGE: One pot lasts four seasons, with yucca and bergenia as the core plants. In spring, pansies and lamium steal the show, while in winter, when the bergenia has died back, stems from yellow- and redtwig dogwoods add to the yucca's colorful display.

Emerald arborvitae

LIGHT:
Full sun to light shade

SIZE:
4 feet wide and 15 feet tall

ZONES:
2–7

Bergenia

LIGHT:
Full sun to light shade

SIZE:
12 to 15 inches tall;
leaves are 6 to 8 inches wide and
10 to 20 inches long

ZONES:
3–8

Golden creeping Jenny is perfect for the edge of the pot

Golden creeping Jenny (*Lysimachia nummularia* 'Aurea', Zones 4–8) is truly a reliable performer in a container. This 4-inch-tall plant cascades beautifully over the rim of a pot. Its golden, coin-shaped leaves look good with everything. It likes partial shade but loves water, so much so that it will grow in a water garden. It can take full sun, too, but you need to keep the soil moist.

Japanese pieris has colorful new growth

This deer-resistant shrub (*Pieris japonica* and cvs., Zones 6–8) is an excellent candidate for containers. Though its evergreen foliage provides interest in all seasons, the spring growth on Japanese pieris is especially striking, depending on the cultivar. In winter, the flower buds are showy— usually dark red, with some opening to shades of pink. Delicate 3- to 6-inch-long racemes of white, urn-shaped blossoms appear in early spring, and they bear a slight fragrance. The graceful branches of this shrub drape naturally over the edges of pots. Compact forms such as 'Dorothy Wyckoff' grow densely so that smaller plants are not always necessary for an attractive container display. Japanese pieris grows in full sun to full shade. Protect it from winter's harsh winds and strong sun.

Variegated redtwig dogwood is big and beautiful

Variegated redtwig dogwood (*Cornus alba* 'Elegantissima', Zones 2–8) performs nicely in containers. Its leaves have white margins and grayish green centers, and the bright red stems shine in winter, particularly if given an evergreen backdrop. A single 'Elegantissima' growing in a 24-inch-wide, blue ceramic pot has worked for three years as a focal point in one of our borders. The shrub's variegated

Golden creeping Jenny

LIGHT:
Partial shade

SIZE:
4 inches tall

ZONES:
4–8

Japanese pieris

LIGHT:
Full sun to full shade

SIZE:
3 to 6 inches long

ZONES:
6–8

leaves are a handsome foil to the hydrangeas in the ground on either side of it, and a mass of variegated Solomon's seal near the base of the container conceals it most of the year. The dogwood's deepest color appears on young stems, so remove old branches in early spring. Place this shrub in full sun to half shade, and watch out for Japanese beetles in summer.

Heucheras provide small spots of interest

Heucheras (*Heuchera* spp. and cvs., Zones 3–8) are attractive, low-growing perennials that excel at providing interest below the taller plants in a container. Their lobed foliage can be showy, often possessing silver veins through green or purple leaves. Heucheras are particularly suited for containers because they like well-drained soil and recover easily from winter. Most heucheras grow into a 12- to 18-inch-diameter mound and toss up flower panicles with white, pink, or red blossoms. They can grow in full sun to full shade, depending on the cultivar.

Variegated redtwig dogwood

LIGHT:
Full sun to partial shade

SIZE:
24 inches wide and to 10 feet tall

ZONES:
2–8

Heucheras

LIGHT:
Full sun to full shade

SIZE:
12- to 18-inch mounds

ZONES:
3–8

Overwintering Plants in a Container

- **SELECT A FROSTPROOF CONTAINER.**
  Choose a pot with a drainage hole in the bottom and made of fiberglass, lead, iron, heavy plastic, or stone. Most terra-cotta will crack in cold temperatures, but you may have luck with glazed pottery.

- **USE A GOOD POTTING SOIL.**
  There are mixes specifically made for use in containers, which provide the essential drainage that plants living in pots need.

- **STOP FEEDING IN FALL.**
  If you use a water-soluble fertilizer, stop feeding your plants about six to eight weeks before your first frost date. This will prevent any tender new growth, which wouldn't survive the winter. Begin fertilizing again when the plants resume growth in the spring.

- **WATER INTO WINTER.**
  Water as needed until the soil in the container is frozen. Do not water frozen pots because the plants are unable to absorb the water.

- **APPLY AN ANTIDESICCANT.**
  Use products such as Wilt-Pruf® on broadleaf evergreens and conifers to protect against damage from winter winds.

- **REPOT EVERY FEW YEARS.**
  Though some plants will live longer in a container, repot your plants every three years to be on the safe side.

Tulips

Iris

Narcissus

Hyacinth

Spring Bulbs in Containers

BY RICHARD HARTLAGE

W HEN I PLANT CONTAINERS OF BULBS IN THE fall at the Elizabeth C. Miller Botanical Garden in Seattle, where I work, I'm thinking of the color and drama they will add to the following spring's landscape. Not only will these planted pots create focal points throughout the garden, but they will also welcome visitors at entryways and add a touch of bright color to the proverbial backdrop of Northwest green.

Any bulb can be planted in a container, but tulips are by far my favorite because of their simple form and the infinite choice of colors. You can combine different types of bulbs in a single container, but be sure they bloom at the same time or the earlier bulb's dying foliage will mar the display of the later-flowering bulb. I prefer to plant only one type of bulb per container to get the maximum impact. By choosing bulbs with staggered bloom times we have a succession of flowers from early March through mid-May.

Plant bulbs in containers in late fall

I plant bulbs in late October in containers with good drainage. In a 24-inch container I plant either 50 tulips, 30 large-flowered daffodils, 50 small-flowered daffodils, or 100 minor bulbs, like *Crocus*, *Muscari*, *Scilla*, or *Iris* species or cultivars. I fill the pot with a soil mix that drains very well so the bulbs will sit in moist but not soggy soil. I plant the bulbs just as I would in the ground, at a soil depth of twice the diameter of the bulb.

If I am planting more than one type of bulb in the same container and they require different planting depths, I layer the bulbs (see p. 138). I fill the container to the right level and plant the larger bulbs, then cover them with soil until it's at the proper depth to plant the smaller bulbs. Finally, I fill the container with soil, being sure to leave at least ½ inch of space between the surface of the soil and the top of the container for easy watering.

I water the planted container thoroughly, then water periodically throughout the winter. The bulbs should not sit in soil that is too wet, but you also don't want them to dry out entirely.

Overwintering methods depend on where you live

Gardening in Seattle makes overwintering bulbs in containers rather easy. I use mostly stoneware pots because they can be left outside through the winter. Our mild winters allow us to group the pots together tightly in our nursery and leave them outside for the season.

More durable containers made of stone, cast concrete, fiberglass, cast iron, or plastic are suitable for colder winter

Plan for a succession of color. When this container of *Tulipa* 'Spring Green' finishes blooming, it will be replaced with another container of tulips just starting to open.

Layering Bulbs in Containers

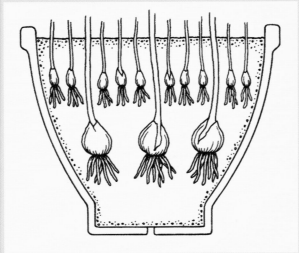

TO PLANT A CONTAINER with different species of bulbs, plant the larger bulbs first, then cover them with soil and plant the smaller bulbs. Fill the container with soil to just below the rim.

An extra-large container of the delicate *Narcissus* 'Hawera' lights up a dark area of the garden. Accompanied by two pots of purple pansies, these containers also mark the transition from the lawn to a stone stairway.

climates. In cold parts of the country, you could surround the pots in tightly packed straw or bury them in sawdust and put a good 18 inches of mulch on top. Or you could store them in a garage or outbuilding that won't get too far below freezing but will also not heat up during the day.

If your winter is just too severe to risk leaving the bulbs out or you want to use bulbs in a container that can't be stored in the cold, you have another option. Plant your bulbs in small 6-or 8-inch plastic pots and overwinter them under protection outdoors (in a

cold frame, for instance) or in a cold garage. In the spring, as they start to bloom, you can then sink the pots into larger display containers. Bring your containers outside in the spring when the danger of hard frost has passed or when the bulbs in the ground are starting to emerge.

After the flowers have faded and the spring gala is over, I plant all the bulbs except for the tulips in the garden. Tulips tend not to do well in subsequent years, so I compost them. Then I start thinking ahead to the varieties I'll be planting up in the fall for next year's display.

Compact roses like 'The Fairy' stay in scale with their containers without the need for heavy pruning. Growing small cultivars in containers prevents them from being overwhelmed by neighboring plants.

Roses for Containers

BY ANDREW SCHULMAN

H UNDREDS OF ROSES ARE CRAMMED INTO MY small urban garden, and since an elaborate deck prevents me from expanding my borders to accommodate new plants, enlarging the collection has become a challenge. Luckily, the deck offers the opportunity for plenty of large decorative containers, which I routinely fill with roses.

Through trial and error, I've discovered that the tricks to growing roses successfully as container plants are to choose those rose varieties best suited to container culture (see "A Few Roses to Consider," p. 143), to start with adequately sized containers, and most important, to follow a few basic cultural principles.

When choosing roses for containers, I look for naturally compact varieties that will stay in scale with their containers without heavy pruning. I also prefer repeat bloomers to maximize seasonal interest. I've had success with compact polyantha roses like 'Baby Faurax' and 'The Fairy' (photo, facing page), while continuously blooming China roses, including 'Ducher', worked just as well. Fragrance is a plus since containers can bring shorter-growing roses closer to the nose.

Most of my favorite container roses, however, lack the vigor and full, bushy habit I prefer in garden roses. Consider 'Rose du Roi', a 19th-century Portland rose that figures in the pedigrees of most modern red roses. 'Rose du Roi' is seldom planted, perhaps because its low, open habit and slow growth make it awkward to place in the mixed border. Ironically, these same traits make 'Rose du Roi' an ideal container plant. The sparse, angular branches leave plenty of room for the plum-and-silver foliage of *Heuchera americana* 'Persian Carpet' (Zones 4–8), which in turn provides a superb foil for the rose's large, flat, crimson flowers. Though even the larger-growing Portland roses like 'Rembrandt' and 'Marchesa Boccella' can make fine container plants, 'Rose du Roi' grows so slowly that it rarely outgrows its pot.

Half whiskey barrels are the perfect size for compact roses like *R.* 'Hermosa'. You may need to treat the barrels with a water-based preservative to prevent the wood from decomposing.

'Kronprincessin Viktoria', a sport of the famous Bourbon rose 'Souvenir de la Malmaison', has stunning, fragrant white flowers. But the plant itself has always struck me as weak and spindly, with stiff canes and a rigid habit. Certain that neighboring border plants would quickly overwhelm it, I tried 'Kronprincessin Viktoria' in a cast-concrete container. To help flesh out the rose's sparse foliage, I paired it with a daylily (*Hemerocallis* 'Frosted Pink Ice', Zones 3–10) known for slow growth and limited clump size. The two now cohabit happily with the deep purple foliage and magenta blooms of *Sedum* 'Vera Jameson' (Zones 4–9) at their feet.

Bigger containers are best

Growing full-size roses and their companion plants together in containers is gardening at its most intensive. An adequately sized container and a few special cultural measures are crucial for success. The smallest container I'll consider for a rose is 20 inches across; 24- to 36-inch-diameter containers are ideal. For durability, I lean toward cast stone or molded resin. While the popular half whiskey barrels are a good size, they tend to decompose in my climate unless heavily treated with preservatives.

No matter what the material, proper drainage is essential. If the containers I choose lack drainage holes, I perforate their bottoms in several places with a power drill fitted with a 1/2-inch bit. The choice of potting soil is also important in maintaining healthy growth. I use a commercial potting mix that includes a high percentage of organic matter, along with plenty of perlite and sharp sand to enhance drainage and air volume. I also repot my roses every three or four years into fresh potting soil. I do this toward the end of winter dormancy, pruning the canes hard and rinsing all of the old soil off the plant's roots. If a plant is root bound, I put it into a larger container and carefully prune away any roots that encircled the old pot. Repotting also gives me the opportunity to divide and move the various perennial companion plants in each container.

Give 'em a drink and keep 'em fed

Container-grown roses dry out quickly and require frequent watering. I check my containers every day during the spring and summer, even if the weather has been rainy. In my experience, natural rainfall is rarely, if ever, sufficient to sustain a rose in a container. Even with automated irrigation, check the soil frequently for moisture, since uptake and evaporation vary considerably during the season.

With such frequent watering, nutrients tend to leach from the soil rapidly, so I apply a water-soluble fertilizer once a week. I begin feeding when growth emerges in the spring and cut back in September so the summer growth can harden off before the first frosts. To supplement the organic content of the soil, I top-dress each container generously with organic compost in autumn. Be sure to avoid overfeeding container-grown roses with high-nitrogen fertilizers, as too

A Few Roses to Consider

CULTIVAR	FLOWER COLOR	GROWTH HABIT*	
Rosa 'Baby Faurax'	mauve	compact	
R. 'Clotilde Soupert'	pale pink	compact	
R. 'Ducher'	white	compact	'Ducher'
R. 'Hermosa'	pink	compact	
R. 'Kronprincessin Viktoria'	white	medium	
R. 'Lady Ann Kidwell'	deep pink	compact	
R. 'Madame Antoine Mari'	cream and pink	medium	
R. 'Marchesa Boccella'	light pink	medium	
R. 'Marie Pavié'	white	compact	'Rise 'n' Shine'
R. 'Mutabilis'	yellow changing to pink	medium	
R. 'Rembrandt'	brick red	medium	
R. 'Rise 'n' Shine'	yellow	compact	
R. 'Rose du Roi'	crimson	compact	
R. 'The Fairy'	light pink	compact	'Valentine'
R. 'Valentine'	red	compact	

* Compact cultivars generally grow no larger than 3 feet tall and wide. Medium cultivars may grow up to 4 feet tall and wide.

much nitrogen will cause excessive leaf growth at the expense of blooms.

Roses in containers are vulnerable to cold. Even here in Zone 8, I coddle my more-tender tea roses by wrapping their containers in a layer of home insulation secured with heavy plastic. By planting in lightweight containers set on wheeled bases, cold-climate gardeners can grow even the most tender tea and China roses. Simply move the containers into shelter at winter's onset.

SOURCES

- Antique Rose Emporium; 800-441-0002; www.antiqueroseemporium.com

- Roses Unlimited; 864-682-7673; www.rosesunlimitedownroot.com

- Vintage Gardens Antique Roses; 707-829-2035; www.vintagegardens.com

Plants, clockwise from top, are *Yucca thompsoniana, Crassula arborescens, Ferocactus latispinus, Mammillaria* spp., *Astrophytum myriostigma,* and *Agave lophantha.*

Sun-Worshipping Plants

BY TOM PEACE

HOT, DRY CLIMATES ARE FOUND AROUND THE world, and the diversity of forms and drought-survival strategies of the plants that thrive in these hot areas boggles my mind and delights my heart. Most of these drought-adapted plants store water in their leaves, stems, or roots, and although there are many plants waiting to be discovered for our garden use, there are lots already available for us to try. A few of these plants are winter hardy, but most are not, so I treat them either as annuals, letting them die at the end of the season, or as tender perennials. As I do with my tender perennials, I bring some of them into the house for the winter, placing them in a sunny spot and watering them infrequently. They never look their best, but they usually make it through to the following spring.

One of the most popular and easy-to-find groups of drought-adapted plants is succulents, which store water in their leaves. This broad group includes the cold-hardy hens-and-chicks (*Sempervivum* spp. and cvs., Zones 4–10) and sedums (*Sedum* spp. and cvs., Zones 4–10) as well as the more tender *Graptopetalum* and *Echeveria* species.

Another easy-to-find group is the large, diverse cactus family, which eschews leaves for succulent stems that hold moisture through dry times. They come in various prickly forms including barrels, pads, mounds, and clumps. There are both cold-hardy species and

more tender types. There are even some tropical cacti. All cacti grow well in containers—just be careful of their spines and of the tiny but more obnoxious glochids, the small clusters of stiff hairs that can get stuck in your skin.

South Africa is home to a host of dry-loving plants, all of which make great container specimens. The ice plant family (Aizoaceae) includes plants like living stones (*Lithops* spp.) and the hardy ice plants (*Delosperma* spp. and cvs.). There are also delightful aloes (*Aloe* spp. and cvs., Zones 10–11) and their cousins from the *Gasteria* and *Haworthia* species, and the long-blooming members of the

Many low-care plants have architectural qualities that allow them to be used as single specimens in a container. LEFT: *Agave gypsophylla* stands alone in an elegant urn; CENTER: a cushion of moss rose fills an old birdbath; RIGHT: *Agave geminiflora* explodes from a terra-cotta pot

---

TIP

Your weather determines your soil mix

If you have dry summers, use a soilless mix that doesn't contain much peat moss, and add perlite or pumice gravel to it. In moist, humid summers, use a soilless mix and add coarse grit or pea gravel because extra drainage is a must. You can also create your own mix of 50 percent pea gravel and 50 percent compost/pine bark. Be aware, however, that this mix will add a lot of weight to your containers.

Note: Don't add moisture-retaining polymer crystals to either of these potting mixes because water-misers like it dry.

Bulbine genus. Another South African plant family (Crassulaceae) includes *Crassula*, *Kalanchoe*, and *Cotyledon*, which come in many shapes, sizes, and colors. There are also bizarre-looking euphorbias (*Euphorbia* spp. and cvs., Zones 4–11) that need little water and are perfect for pot culture.

Closer to home, in the desert Southwest of North America, are drought-adapted plants like *Agave*, *Yucca*, and *Dasylirion* species and cultivars, bear grasses (*Nolina* spp.), and ponytail palms (*Beaucarnea* spp.), all of which sport tough, leathery leaves that are sometimes far from succulent yet are adapted to withstand dry conditions. These woody lilies, as they are sometimes called, hold moisture through dry times, and some are also quite cold hardy, ranging from Zone 5 to Zone 9.

The Americas are also home to a wealth of bromeliads, including *Puya*, *Hechtia*, and *Dyckia* species. With their drought tolerance and their strange and spiny starfishlike appearance, they make delightful container specimens that are worth looking for.

Finally, a plant that can be found in almost every nursery is the floriferous annual moss rose (*Portulaca grandiflora* cvs.), which is tolerant of both heat and drought. Available in a range of colors including white, yellow, pink, magenta, orange, and peach, it makes a colorful addition to containers with other specimens and plays a supporting role under the larger horticultural stars.

LEFT: This golden barrel cactus (*Echinocactus grusonii*) thrives in dry weather. A Russian sage (*Perovskia* 'Hybrida') blooms in the background.

RIGHT: Lining the path in this dry-loving garden are, front to back, *Cleistocactus winteri, Dasylirion acrotriche,* and *Agave angustifolia.*

Also, in the same family, the genus *Talinum* contains several colorful species well adapted to pot life, including 'Jewels-of-Opar', which comes in both variegated-leaf and chartreuse forms.

All of these plants perform well during dry periods. This makes them the perfect container plants for busy gardeners who don't always have time to give their plants a cool drink.

SOURCES

The following mail-order nurseries offer large selections of plants for xeric containers.

- Bob Smoley's Gardenworld; 724-443-6770; www.bobsmoleys.com

- High Country Gardens; 800-925-9387; www.highcountrygardens.com

- Yucca Do Nursery; 979-826-4580; www.yuccado.com

LEFT: A harmonious grouping of plants includes, clockwise from top right: *Aloe cryptopoda, Agave murpheyi* 'Variegata', *Agave victoriae-reginae,* and *Yucca whipplei.*

RIGHT: The author has adorned his pachypodium with blue marbles, which draw attention to its spiny trunk.

If you have something that holds water, like this kettledrum, you can have a water garden.

Water-Loving Plants

BY GREG SPEICHERT

ATER FEATURES IN A GARDEN ROOM OR patio instantly create a peaceful feeling and say that there is something special and distinct about the place. Water brings the light down from the sky and reflects it back to us. It heightens plants' textures and enhances their forms. Best of all, it opens up a new world of plants for us to grow. But who wants to excavate for a pond or run electricity for a pump and filter? Adding a water feature to your garden usually takes time, money, and effort.

The solution is a water container. Find any object that can hold water and fill it up. You have just created an environment that will do all the wonderful things water does for a garden. Once you've set up a container (see "Water Container Basics", p. 152), the fun part is next: choosing the plants.

As with any container combination, water containers need a mixture of upright, bushy, and creeping plants to look balanced. The plants here fit into these categories and can be combined with one another to create beautiful compositions. Each plant also has a stature and habit that work well in a container environment. Most are easily overwintered indoors, too, or you can grow them as annuals, tossing them onto the compost pile at season's end.

Dwarf umbrella grasses
Cyperus alternifolius and cvs.

LIGHT:
Part sun to shade

SIZE:
2 to 4 feet tall and 1 to 2 feet wide

WATER DEPTH:
Up to 4 inches above the crown

Dwarf umbrella grasses

Umbrella grasses (*Cyperus alternifolius* and cvs., syn. *C. involucratus*, Zones 9–11) usually grow up to 6 feet tall, but several dwarf cultivars are perfect for water containers. Their upright habit and long, narrow leaves add height and grace to a composition. 'Gracilis' retains the elegance of its taller cousins while reaching only 2 feet high and 1 foot wide. 'Variegatus' is as tall as 'Gracilis' but is twice as wide. As its name suggests, 'Variegatus' has striking green-and-white variegated leaves, but they often suddenly revert to all green. 'Nanus', which grows from 2 to 4 feet tall, is the biggest of the umbrella grasses I would recommend for a container.

Dwarf umbrella grasses are naturally yellow-green. The more sun they get, the more yellow their leaves become, especially if you don't feed the plant enough. If you want to be sure a plant stays green, give it morning sun and fertilize it regularly. Since dwarf umbrella grasses get tall, grow them in pots that are at least 1 gallon or larger so that they don't fall over. If the plant is not hardy in your area, bring it indoors during the colder months and set it in a tray of water.

Dwarf parrot feather

The common parrot feather (*Myriophyllum aquaticum*, Zones 6–11) is a mainstay of water gardens and with good reason. Its soft, furry plumes are small but plentiful, and the fine texture makes an impact. Dwarf parrot feather (*Myriophyllum papillosum* var. *pulcherrima*, Zones 6–11) is a more refined relative of the common species and is perfect for water containers because it gets only half as tall (4 inches) as its ubiquitous cousin.

Dwarf parrot feather needs only a small, 4-inch-diameter pot in which to grow, but it will spread over the surface of the water, hiding the pots of other plants and spilling over the edge of the container. Because it will float, dwarf parrot feather can be grown in deep water; just don't submerge it. This plant grows easily from stem cuttings. Simply take a bunch of it and add it to another pot in the container, or clip it to the side of the container. Overwintering cuttings in the house is just as easy.

Dwarf parrot feather
Myriophyllum papillosum var. *pulcherrima*

LIGHT:
Sun to shade

SIZE:
4 inches high and an indefinite spread

WATER DEPTH:
As deep as you can go
without submerging the entire plant

Water Container Basics

WHILE ANY CONTAINER THAT HOLDS WATER can become a water container, choose one with a suitable depth for the plants you will be growing. Use the size of your largest plant as a guide, and make sure that the container can provide the right depth. Smaller plants can be set on stones or bricks to raise them up.

If your perfect container has a hole in the bottom, put tape across the bottom of the hole, then plug the hole from the inside with plumber's putty. A container made from a porous material like terra-cotta will need to have a sealant applied before it will hold water.

You won't need a pump, since container water gardens hold a small amount of water; in the unlikely event you get algae or mosquitoes, just dump out the container and add fresh water. Or you can simply overflow the container every time you add water, removing anything growing on or near the surface. Stagnancy shouldn't be a concern because the water is constantly being refreshed due to evaporation and plant use.

When planting, place plants in the container, keeping them in their original pots. If the pots do not have a top layer of pea gravel, add one to prevent soil leakage, which would dirty the water. Be sure to set plants at the proper depth as you arrange them.

Use a fertilizer intended for water plants because conditions underwater are different from those underground. Feed your plants monthly until the water reaches about 80°F and then fertilize every two weeks.

Corkscrew rush

Corkscrew rush (*Juncus effusus* 'Spiralis', Zones 6–9) has tightly coiled foliage whose upright form is perfect for containers. I like this rush because it is more interesting than those with straight foliage—and in a small container, you need plenty of interest. Since corkscrew rush doesn't like to have its crown submerged in the summer, position the plant so that its crown sits just above the water. Because it's a grass, it needs to be fed to stay green; otherwise, it will turn yellow and fail to grow. The foliage will kink if it gets manhandled, so if the dog likes to drink from your container, avoid this plant.

'Crushed Ice' arrowhead

The bold foliage and clean white flowers of arrowheads (*Sagittaria* spp. and cvs., Zones 5–11) make them great plants for water containers. Easy to grow in sun to light shade, they are rampant runners and can fill a container. Growing them in a 1-gallon pot will keep them in check and also make the plant look fuller. Arrowheads are heavy feeders. To keep them green, growing, and flowering in a small container, give them frequent doses of a fertilizer designed for water plants.

Arrowheads vary widely in height and leaf shape. I like 'Crushed Ice' arrowhead (*Sagittaria graminea* 'Crushed Ice') for a container because it is a great bloomer and gets only 1 foot tall and 1 foot wide. Best of all are the slender, variegated leaves that are in proportion to a container but still provide visual interest. Where the summers get hot and humid, 'Crushed Ice' will benefit from afternoon shade.

'Crushed Ice' arrowhead
Sagittaria graminea 'Crushed Ice'

LIGHT:
Sun to light shade

SIZE:
1 foot tall and wide

WATER DEPTH:
Up to 1 inch above the crown

Water clovers
Marsilea spp. and cvs.

LIGHT:
Sun to shade

SIZE:
¼ inch to 6 inches tall with
an indeterminate spread

WATER DEPTH:
Up to 4 inches above the crown

Water clovers

The aptly named water clovers (*Marsilea* spp. and cvs., Zones 6–11) have attractive foliage that insinuates itself in and around the other plants in the container. As an added feature, the leaves close at night and resemble little butterflies sleeping on the water. These plants grow in sun or shade and are easy to care for, requiring only occasional feeding and thinning. Don't worry about over thinning—they don't mind a touch of ruthlessness when you cut them back. Many water clovers are hardy to Zone 6, but all are easy to grow indoors if need be. Because they grow from creeping rhizomes, any piece that has roots and a leaf will grow.

Yellow monkey flower

Yellow monkey flower (*Mimulus guttatus* and cvs., syn. *M. langsdorfii*, Zones 6–9) is a summer bloomer that likes a little shade. Reaching anywhere from 2 to 10 inches tall, it subtly weaves its way among other plants in the container, adding a touch of color. If you deadhead and feed this plant steadily throughout the summer, it will keep producing 1½-inch-long yellow flowers. It does best in shallow, moving water, especially when the water temperature rises above 65°F. If you don't have a pump, yellow monkey flower will still do fine.

Choosing Soil for Water Containers

WHEN IT COMES TO CHOOSING THE BEST potting medium for aquatic plants, there is no one right answer. Ideally, the medium should supply anchorage, fertilization, and moisture retention. The potting mix should also suit the needs of the gardener. It should be easy to use, odorless, and not make the pond look muddy. Affordability and availability are also important factors. Here are a few of the best options.

Clay soil

Clay soil holds water and nutrients and effectively anchors plants in place. However, clay soil makes pond water muddy when disturbed.

Kitty litter

While kitty liter isn't a potting medium, it's as good as clay soil at holding nutrients and moisture. It won't muddy pond water if disturbed. Look for brands made from calcified clay because it's not chemically treated or deodorized. Avoid products that contain shredded paper or other nonclay materials.

Sand

A good medium for short plants with creeping habits is sand (tall plants potted in sand tend to fall over). Sand doesn't hold nutrients as well as clay soil does, so plants potted in sand need to be fertilized regularly.

Cocoa fiber

Filtration plants love to be planted in cocoa fiber because it acts like pea gravel and allows water to flow through a plant's roots. Tall plants often fall over when planted in cocoa fiber, so pots will need to be weighted.

Pebbles and pea gravel

The ideal media for potting filtration plants, pebbles and pea gravel allow the roots of aquatic plants to catch nutrients as they pass through the crevices created by the small stones. If you use this as your potting medium, you'll want to include filtration plants—like rushes, reeds, and pickerelweeds—to absorb nutrients from the water.

Yellow monkey flower
Mimulus guttatus and cvs.

LIGHT:
Part sun to shade

SIZE:
Up to 10 inches tall and wide

WATER DEPTH:
Up to the crown or
1 inch above in summer

Ornamental millet
Pennisetum glaucum 'Purple Majesty'

LIGHT:
Full sun

SIZE:
3 to 4 feet tall and 1 foot wide

ANNUAL

Several spikes of ornamental millet shoot skyward above a similarly hued Persian shield (*Strobilanthes dyerianus*, Zones 9–11); 'Orange Zest' salvia (*Salvia splendens* 'Orange Zest', annual); and cascading, yellow-flowered toothache plant (*Spilanthes acmella*, Zones 10–11).

A Gallery of Three Fundamental Plants

BY FINE GARDENING EDITORS

THERE'S NO MYSTERY IN MAKING A SCRUMPTIOUS container planting as long as you follow a simple three-ingredient recipe. First and foremost, you start with a "thriller": a centerpiece plant with star quality, something big, bold, and beautiful. Then you add a few spicy "fillers"—foliage or flowering plants that will complement, but not overwhelm, the main player. Finally, you add a savory splash of mischief, a "spiller" that just tumbles out of the pot. Combining thrillers, fillers, and spillers creates a lush, intriguing composition rich in color, texture, and form. It fills out a pot by exploiting space in every available direction—up, down, and sideways. By using at least one of each of these kinds of plants in various proportions and by taking care to balance colors and textures, you can create a pot with pizzazz.

When selecting plants, you should consider the element of scale. Start with the size of the pot. Bigger pots need bigger plants, while smaller pots—those less than 12 inches in diameter—provide a chance to create micro compositions using tiny plants. And always consider how the pot will be viewed. If it will be seen from all sides, position your thriller in the center and work around it. But if the pot goes against a wall or in a border where it will be seen from only one side, put the thriller toward the back of the pot, which will give you more room up front to play with a greater variety of fillers and spillers.

Also bear in mind that the boundaries between these three basic plant types aren't fixed. Depending on the arrangement and scale of a planting, some fillers—especially if they are large—might get promoted to thrillers; some fillers might spill a bit; and some thrillers might serve as fillers when paired with something larger and more exotic.

Thrillers make a bold and exciting centerpiece

Angelonias are true flower-ing machines, producing spire after blossom-covered spire in a season-long display of color. Depending on the cul-tivar, angelonias boast clusters of flowers in flawless shades of white, pinks, purples, a range of purple-kissed blues, and a bicolor or two. Whatever their color, they love being part of the gang in large mixed containers. Though it's not necessary, a little manicuring helps these vigorous plants produce the most blooms and look their best. The best form and flowers result from plants that have been deadheaded. Luckily, that's a breeze—just cut back any tired-looking flower stalks to their base.

New Zealand flax is a container must-have for its handsome, blade-like foliage and gracious, mounding habit. The leaves are especially valu-able because each blade is rather wide, providing a commanding presence. Few plants grab your attention as effectively as a spiky swarm of New Zealand flaxes jutting from a pot. There are a whole slew of color variations available, rang-ing from greenish yellow to pink-tinged and on to sultry burgundy. They are best for climates with cooler summers and are fine as specimens grown in pots by themselves.

New Zealand flax
Phormium spp. and cvs.

LIGHT:
Full sun

SIZE:
Up to 4 feet tall and
4 feet wide

ZONES:
8–11

Angelonia
Angelonia angustifolia cvs.

LIGHT:
Full sun

SIZE:
18 to 24 inches tall and
12 inches wide

ZONES:
9–10

Angelface® Pink angelonia shares the thriller spotlight with spiky blue mealy-cup sage (*Salvia farinacea,* Zones 8–11). The purple ageratum (*Ageratum houstonianum* cv., annual) serves as an understated filler, while a white calibrachoa (*Calibrachoa* cv., annual) spills over the edge.

Cordyline
Cordyline australis cvs.

LIGHT:
Full sun to partial shade

SIZE:
Up to 6 feet tall and
3 feet wide

ZONES:
10–11

A separate pot allows this
'Red Sensation' cordyline to
shine next to a variegated
shell ginger (*Alpinia zerumbet*
'Variegata', Zones 8–11)
without crowding it.

Colorful **cordyline cultivars**
are a vast improvement over the plain
old green dracaena spike (*Cordyline australis*, Zones 10–11), which has been a
container ingredient since, it seems, the
days of the Roman Empire. I usually forgo using fillers with younger plants. With
age, cordylines develop a long, bare stem
that affords plenty of room for fillers
such as wild petunia (*Petunia intregrifolia*,
annual), golden jewels of Opar (*Talinum
paniculatum* 'Kingwood Gold', annual),
and pouch flowers (*Calceolaria* spp. and
cvs., annual). Just about any lantana or
nasturtium will do as a spiller, or for a
more colorful splash, tuck in a Brazilian
firecracker (*Manettia luteorubra*,
Zone 11).

For a jolt of easy-growing tropical
drama, **elephant ears** deliver. Their
welcome mat–size leaves come in an
alluring variety of colors, such as the
deep burgundy-black of C. *esculenta*
'Black Magic' and the dark-leaved,
chartreuse-veined C. *esculenta* 'Illustris'.
As if the dramatic colors and shapes
weren't enough, the broad leaves sway
seductively in the breeze, adding an
extra touch of tropicality. That said,
it can be a challenge to use elephant
ears in mixed containers. They grow
so rapidly that they can overrun any
companion plantings. I often grow
elephant ears in a pot of their own,
then combine them with groupings of
other potted plants.

Elephant ears

Colocasia esculenta and cvs.,
Xanthosoma spp. and cvs., and
Alocasia spp. and cvs.

LIGHT:
Partial shade

SIZE:
Up to 5 feet tall and wide

ZONES:
8–11

A. macrorrhiza

C. esculenta 'Illustris'

C. esculenta 'Black Magic'

Upright fuchsia
Fuchsia spp. and cvs.

LIGHT:
Partial shade

SIZE:
Up to 3 feet tall and
2 feet wide

ZONES:
9–11

When one thinks of **fuchsias,** hanging baskets often come to mind. But there's another branch in the fuchsia family tree, one that tends to grow up rather than down. These shrubby, upright fuchsias reach for the sky with flair. Like their recumbent cousins, they are tireless, colorful bloomers. Some have nodding flowers that wouldn't put anyone to sleep. Others bear tiny trumpets that send a siren call to hummingbirds. A few, such as *F. magellanica* 'Aurea', bear gaily bright foliage, while others, such as 'Gartenmeister Bonstedt' (left) and 'Coralle', sport smoky leaves that harmonize with a host of hot colors.

Bamboo
Bambusa spp. and cvs.,
Fargesia spp. and cvs.,
and *Phyllostachys* spp. and cvs.

LIGHT:
Full sun to partial shade

SIZE:
Up to 30 feet tall with an
indefinite spread

ZONES:
5–11

Big, bold, and airy all at once, **bamboos** are a singular thriller, one that is soft yet sturdy. They're grasses with backbone. My favorite bamboo for containers is black-stemmed bamboo (*Phyllostachys nigra* var. *henonis*, Zones 7–11) because the visible stems provide a structural skeleton to the bamboo's leafy froth. Bold, rounded foliage makes a good counterpoint to bamboo's delicate, linear leaves. I like 'Green and Gold' plectranthus (*Plectranthus discolor* 'Green and Gold', Zones 10–11) as a filler and golden sweet potato vine (*Ipomoea batatas* 'Margarita', Zone 11) as a spiller.

Persian shield
Strobilanthes dyerianus

LIGHT:
Full sun to partial shade

SIZE:
Up to 4 feet tall and
3 feet wide

ZONES:
9–11

In this plush pot of purple, New Wonder® scaevola (*Scaevola aemula* 'New Wonder') plays both filler and spiller to the thriller, Persian shield.

The silver-coated, pinky purples of **Persian shield's** leaves combine with a surprising array of warm and cool colors. This goof-proof plant is a reliably good grower, a great thriller, and a fine filler. It's a challenge to find a color that Persian shield does not flatter, but it looks best with pinks, blues, and purples.

Combine it with any silver-foliaged plant. Or go for eye-popping pizzazz by adding chartreuse. Alternatively, rein things in with subdued burgundy foliage. The plant's sole drawback is its tendency to look washed out if grown in a location that is too shady; full sun yields the most vivid colors.

> ### Honey bush
> *Melianthus major*
>
> **LIGHT:**
> Full sun
>
> **SIZE:**
> 5 feet tall and
> wide
>
> **ZONES:**
> 8–11

Spillers tumble
from the container

Honey bush has exquisite foliage; its leaves are neatly notched like an alligator's teeth. The leaves and the sturdy branches are a lustrous glaucous shade. A shrub in its native South Africa, honey bush is at once bold and sculptural, delicate and refined. It makes an ideal centerpiece for mixed container plantings, providing a calming focal point and a complement to colors hot, cold, or in between. It also succeeds on its own, planted in a favorite pot where its crisply folded, elegantly serrated foliage can be savored. Give it moist, fertile, well-drained soil.

The beauteous blues of **lobelia** bring to mixed containers a hard-to-find, easy-to-use color. And even better, they bring their hues by way of clouds of tiny little flowers, so the effect is rich with texture, too. If blue is not your thing, there are also lobelias in reds, whites, and lilacs. Because these plants are modest in size, they are especially suited for smaller containers or contrasting larger companions.

Lobelia

Lobelia erinus cvs.

SIZE:
4 to 6 inches tall and
trailing to 8 inches

LIGHT:
Full sun to partial shade

ANNUAL

The compelling blue of
'Regatta Saphire' lobelia
adorns the edge of a pot that
includes 'Inky Fingers' coleus
(*Solenostemon scutellarioides*
'Inky Fingers', Zone 11),
purple fountain grass
(*Pennisetum setaceum* 'Rubrum',
Zones 8–11), and the citrusy
blooms of 'Pin-Up Flame'
tuberous begonia (*Begonia*
'Pin-Up Flame', not hardy
below Zone 11).

'Margarita'

'Tricolor'

Sweet potato vine
Ipomoea batatas cvs.

SIZE:
Up to 10 inches tall and trailing
to 36 or more inches

LIGHT:
Full sun

ZONE:
11

'Sweet Caroline Red'

'Sweet Caroline™ Green Yellow'

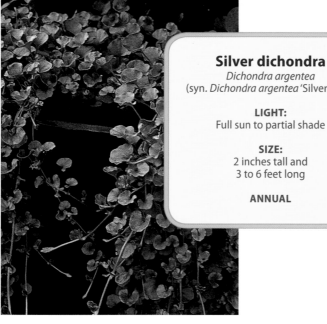

Finely textured **bacopa** is ideal at the edge of a pot, where it will flower non-stop, producing clouds of tiny blossoms. I think it works best when paired with bolder flowers or foliage that provide an echo of the bacopa's hue. Years of breeding have yielded low-maintenance selections for virtually every color scheme. My favorites include 'Cabana Trailing Blue', 'Gold 'n Pearls', and Snowstorm® Pink.

Strung like strands of shiny coins, the rounded metallic leaves of **Silver dichondra,** also called silver ponyfoot, dangle from slender silver-white threads. The stems grow up to 6 feet long, draping themselves over the rims of their containers. It's native to the southwestern United States and to Mexico, but it also thrives in humid regions as long as it's in well-drained soil.

Sweet potato vines can take their place among the best foliage spillers. Perhaps their greatest attribute is their colorful, hand-size leaves, making them among the few fillers featuring bold foliage. Easy to grow and prolific, sweet potato vines come in a host of great colors. If sweet potato vines have a fault, it is that their near-rampant growth means they might occasionally over-run their container companions. That problem has been solved in recent years with the development of more-compact forms with heart-shaped leaves, such as chartreuse Sweet Heart Light Green™ and burgundy Sweet Heart Purple™, or with fleur-de-lis–shaped leaves, such as bronze-hued 'Sweet Caroline Red' or chartreuse 'Sweet Caroline Light Green'.

Supertunia®
Royal Velvet petunia
Petunia 'Kakegawa S28'

LIGHT:
Full sun

SIZE:
6 to 10 inches tall and wide

ANNUAL

Whirlwind®
Blue fan flower
Scaevola aemula 'Scablhatis'

LIGHT:
Partial shade

SIZE:
8 to 12 inches tall
and wide

ANNUAL

This vigorous, ever-blooming trailer has large, velvety, and sweetly fragrant purple flowers that attract butterflies and hummingbirds. Plants can grow up to 1 inch a day, and they "self-clean" by shedding spent flowers. **Supertunia Royal Velvet** is ideal for baskets, window boxes, and patio containers. Plant in moist, well-drained soil. Apply a time-release plant food at planting, or feed monthly with a water-soluble fertilizer.

A patented hybrid of the Australian fan flower, **Whirlwind Blue** blooms from early spring through winter and has attractive emerald green foliage. It looks delicate, but the hybrid is a tough, full-sun trooper that endures stress without leaf loss. Whirlwind Blue likes fertile, humus-rich, moist, well-drained soil.

Like blood leafs or coleus, **alternantheras** are great foliage plants, ideal for weaving among their neighbors and toppling over the edge of a pot. And they are a wonderful find for those seeking dark burgundy or reddish hues, colors in which this plant family seems to specialize. There are also some choice chartreuse shades. These plants like plenty of moisture and will suffer if allowed to get thirsty. They go with almost anything but are exceptional with bananas, cannas, and dahlias.

A. ficoidea 'Bettzichiana'

A. dentata 'Rubiginosa'

Alternanthera
Alternanthera spp. and cvs.

LIGHT:
Full sun to partial shade

SIZE:
Up to 12 inches tall and
trailing indefinitely

ZONES:
9–11

A. ficoidea 'Red Threads'

A. ficoidea 'Golden Threads'

'Blue Eyes' cup flower
Nierembergia 'Blue Eyes'

LIGHT:
Full sun

SIZE:
8 to 10 inches tall
and wide

HARDINESS:
Tender perennial

If you're looking for a flower with a hint of blue, this long-blooming cup flower makes a good compact candidate for a sunny planter. White, five-petaled flowers are centered in yellow with a deep blue ring that radiates through each petal. 'Blue Eyes' blooms from late spring until frost and tolerates dry conditions.

Dragon Wing™ Pink begonia
Begonia Dragon Wing™ Pink

LIGHT:
Sun or shade

SIZE:
15 to 18 inches tall
and wide

ANNUAL

The name for this strain of hybrid begonia—Dragon Wing Pink—comes from its leaves, which are shaped like a wing. The leaves are a bright glossy green, gently pleated, and held on sturdy, succulent stems. Early in June, the stems begin to produce loose flower sprays in endless succession. Flowers and foliage are balanced; the two mingle comfortably, with flowers rising above the leaves and vice versa. Heat tolerant, dragon wing pink needs regular watering and an occasional dousing with a liquid fertilizer.

Fillers fill up the pot

Most agapanthus have blue or white blossoms with green foliage, but this distinctive beauty boasts dark purple blooms on almost-black stems. Everything about 'Back in Black' is striking—even its late-season black seed pods. Feed this dramatic plant with liquid fertilizer if you'll be keeping it in the same pot for several years. Outdoors, it prefers fertile, moist, well-drained soil.

'Back in Black' agapanthus
Agapanthus 'Back in Black'

LIGHT:
Full sun

SIZE:
26 inches tall and
12 inches wide

ZONES:
6-9

Diamond Frost® euphorbia
Euphorbia Diamond Frost®

LIGHT:
Full sun to partial shade

SIZE:
Up to 14 inches tall
and wide

ZONES:
10–11

In this combination, Diamond Frost euphorbia is a sparkling accent to the spikes of English Butterfly Peacock™ butterfly bush (*Buddleia davidii* English Butterfly Peacock™, Zones 5–9), the chartreuse bracts of Kalipso™ euphorbia (*Euphorbia* Kalipso™, Zones 6–11), the fun foliage of 'Merlin's Magic' coleus (*Solenostemon scutellarioides* 'Merlin's Magic', Zone 11), and the soft pink blooms of diascia (*Diascia* cv., Zones 8–9).

> **Lantana**
> *Lantana camara* cvs.
>
> **LIGHT:**
> Full sun
>
> **SIZE:**
> Up to 2 feet tall
> and wide
>
> **ZONE:**
> 11

Diamond Frost looks like dwarf baby's breath (*Gypsophila elegans* and cvs., Zones 5–9), but its delicate cloud of tiny white blossoms lasts all season long. Plants form a tidy dome and are rugged enough to withstand dry situations. For a white scheme, pair it with white angelonia (*Angelonia angustifolia* Angelface® White, Zones 9–10) and silver plectranthus (*Plectranthus argentatus*, Zones 10–11) or an English ivy (*Hedera helix* cvs., Zones 5–11) with white variegation.

Lantanas produce abundant, intriguingly textured flowers and berrylike seedpods. They tend to straddle the line between filler and spiller, with many cultivars spreading out, then drooping down. That makes them especially useful in combinations with low-to-the-ground, spreading thrillers like young cordylines (*Cordyline australis* cvs., Zones 10–11). I prefer hot-colored lantanas for my tropically inspired themes, and for some reason, they are the ones that seem to be most readily available. For more-mannered schemes, there are subtly colored selections in soft hues of pink, pastel yellow, lavender, and yellow-centered white.

Wax begonia
Begonia spp. and cvs.

LIGHT:
Full sun to partial shade

SIZE:
Up to 1 foot tall
and wide

ZONE:
11

Wax, or bedding, **begonias** are diminutive little flower factories with all the vigor of the Energizer Bunny®. Depending on the variety, they produce clusters of smallish, yellow-centered blossoms in shades of white through pink and on to red. Their glossy, rounded leaves come in shades of green or bronze. Carefree and compact, wax begonias have earned a reputation as garden workhorses and are able supporting players. They make fabulous, colorful skirts for thrillers in like-minded colors, such as 'Scarlet Fever' curcuma (*Curcuma* 'Scarlet Fever', Zones 8–11) and cannas (*Canna* spp. and cvs., Zones 8–11).

Like some cosmic force, **pentas** continually generate colorful galaxies of tiny, starlike flowers. These are convivial plants happy to associate with a vast array of partners. They are excellent for creating color echoes with appropriately hued coleus (*Solenostemon scutellarioides* cvs., Zone 11). Try them alongside Persian shield (*Strobilanthes dyerianus*, Zones 9–11), dark-leaved cannas (*Canna* spp. and cvs., Zones 8–11), or 'Red Russian' kale (*Brassica oleracea* 'Red Russian', annual). Finish off these combinations with a spiller like dichondra (*Dichondra argentea* 'Silver Falls', Zones 10–11). In a smaller pot, pentas also make a great thriller.

Pentas
Pentas spp. and cvs.

LIGHT:
Full sun

SIZE:
18 to 36 inches tall and
half as wide

ZONE:
11

Croton
Codiaeum spp. and cvs.

LIGHT:
Full sun to partial shade

SIZE:
Up to 5 feet tall
and wide

ZONE:
11

Tukana® White is among the whitest, most floriferous **verbenas** to be found. Flowering begins in June and continues until the first frosts. The blooms are plentiful but not clotted, creating a fresh, exuberant effect: Think of crisp clouds hovering above dark green mountains. A strawberry jar will disappear beneath this plant's flowers. Give Tukana White regular moisture and feeding.

The glossy leaves of **crotons** are emblazoned with a fiery array of reds, oranges, and yellows, all thrown together with swirls, whorls, splashes, and blots. Some also bear a patchwork of green. Whatever their color, the leaves can be broad, narrow, or curvy like an Indonesian dagger. They're a perfect match for tropical hibiscus (*Hibiscus* spp. and cvs., Zones 10–11), 'Maurelii' banana (*Ensete ventricosum* 'Maurelii', Zones 9–11), and angels' trumpets (*Brugmansia* spp. and cvs., Zone 11). Spillers in colors just as vivid include golden creeping Jenny (*Lysimachia nummularia* 'Aurea', Zones 4–8) and 'Red Threads' alternanthera (*Alternanthera ficoidea* 'Red Threads', Zones 9–11).

Tukana White verbena
Verbena 'Tukana White'

LIGHT:
Full sun

SIZE:
8 inches tall and
12 inches wide

ANNUAL

Dusty miller
Centaurea cineraria 'Colchester White'

LIGHT:
Full sun

SIZE:
Up to 3 feet tall
and wide

ZONES:
7–11

A towering giant salvia
(*Brillantaisia subulugurica*,
Zones 10–11) is skirted by a
gleaming mound of dusty
miller and the pink blooms of
'Butterfly Deep Pink' pentas
(*Pentas* 'Butterfly Deep Pink',
not hardy below Zone 11).

Dusty miller contributes inviting texture and unexpected color to containers. Its filigree of foliage just begs to be touched and is so lacy it almost tickles your eyes. Then there's its ghostly color. I've never known a leaf that could be so white and still grow. Go for a dramatic look by pairing it with black-leaved shooting star (*Pseuderanthemum atropurpureum* 'Rubrum', not hardy below Zone 11) and perhaps a dark coleus like 'Black Velvet' (*Solenostemon scutellarioides* 'Black Velvet', Zone 11). Placed near the edge of a pot, this dusty miller will spill, too.

White blooms rimmed in rich purple adorn the heat-loving **'Balboa Blue Rim' lisianthus**. A narrow, upright plant with silvery green foliage crowned by roselike flowers, 'balboa blue rim' is as suitable for containers as it is for cut arrangements. Plant it in fertile, moist, and well-drained soil. Lisianthus is native to the American Southwest, but this variety comes from Central America.

'Balboa Blue Rim' lisianthus
Lisianthus 'Balboa Blue Rim'

LIGHT:
Full sun to partial shade

SIZE:
18 to 22 inches tall and 8 to 10 inches wide

ANNUAL

PART

3

Materials & Techniques

When watering be sure to soak the soil and avoid the plant itself.

Maintenance Tips for Healthy Containers

BY ANDREA ALBERT

I FEEL LIKE A KID IN A CANDY STORE AS I WANDER AROUND the patio garden outside our condominium. Vines climb trellises and weave through lattice fencing. Blooming annuals and perennials spill out of pots. In all, about 50 containers—mostly huge—brim with luscious plants. To keep my garden from falling into disarray or taking over my life, I follow these seven simple maintenance tips. After all, I'd rather enjoy the garden's beauty than wrestle with a garden hose.

Clean pots to deter disease

A good maintenance routine starts with well-prepared containers. To avoid promoting disease, I thoroughly scrub all previously used pots with dish soap and hot water. Then I sterilize them with a mixture of two parts white vinegar and one part water with a handful of kosher rock salt. You can also use a 10 percent bleach solution. To sterilize small pots, I run them through the dishwasher after cleaning off the debris, then plant in them while they're still damp.

Water soil, not plants

Using a garden hose is the easiest way to water pots. I attach a long-handled wand with a flat, brass rose, which lets me water evenly and reach under plant leaves. Since many plants, especially those with fuzzy leaves, resent having their foliage wet, I water directly into the soil if possible. If there's no spigot handy, a 2-gallon (or larger) watering can with an extended wand works well.

I check the moisture of the soil in each pot daily, at the edges and near the center. I prefer watering those in need of moisture early in the day when it's cool. If any leaves get wet, the sun and wind helps dry them. If I water in the evening, I vigilantly avoid getting leaves wet, since plants are more susceptible to fungal diseases if foliage stays wet overnight.

In summer, I water every day. To wet plant roots thoroughly, I water the pot, let the water soak in until it drains, and then refill the pot. If a plant wilts from lack of water, I immerse the entire pot in tepid water until no air bubbles appear, then place the pot in a shady spot until the plant revives. In spring and fall, I let most plants nearly dry out between waterings.

Keep Pests at Bay

To deter many insects and diseases, place unpeeled garlic cloves an inch deep in the soil near the rim of each pot—about three cloves in a 14-inch-diameter pot. They sprout thin leaves that resemble crocus foliage.

Ensure good drainage

Whatever size the container, good drainage keeps roots from getting soggy, which can lead to root rot. To remedy poor drainage:

- Add extra holes to a pot using an electric drill with a masonry bit.
- Elevate the pots to ensure not only good drainage but also air circulation for the roots. I place small pieces of wood or terra-cotta "feet" under each container. Never put outdoor pots in saucers because stagnant water can cause pest outbreaks and root rot. Recently, my husband built plant stands with slatted openings, which allow pots to drip directly onto our brick patio floor.
- Make a drainage layer—from ½ inch deep for small pots to 2 inches deep for large ones—in the bottom of pots using washed marble chips, pottery shards, or polystyrene "peanuts."
- Add a layer of mulch made of cedar-bark chips or place washed pebbles on the soil's surface to help the soil retain moisture, keep plant roots cool, and prevent splashing when watering. I never fill a pot to more than an inch below its rim so that water and soil don't spill over the edges during watering.

Use big pots

I prefer to use big pots when creating my lush, dramatic displays. Big pots not only give my plants more room for root growth but also need to be watered less often. And, since large containers can be heavy, I place them on dollies to move them easily.

Give 'em air

To ensure ample air circulation, I arrange pots with at least 2 inches between plants. After a heavy rain, I sometimes even rig up oscillating fans to blow-dry the leaves of tuberous begonias, roses, and caladiums.

Fertilize in the morning

Fertilizing during the extreme heat of the day can harm plants, so I fertilize in the morning after watering, usually when it's overcast.

Depending on the plant's needs, I use water-soluble plant food or organic fertilizers such as fish emulsion, liquid kelp, and blood meal, following product instructions. In general, I fertilize once every 7 to 10 days during the growing season. By mid-August, I stop feeding roses, perennials, and other plants I plan to overwinter. Once a month, after watering, I feed all my plants with a solution of ½ cup Epsom salts per gallon of tepid water. For a 22-inch-diameter pot, I add about 1 quart of this mixture. These dissolved crystals of hydrated magnesium sulfate invigorate plants and intensify bloom and fragrance.

Deadhead and prune

I keep plants shapely by trimming excess growth. I also prune all diseased, dead, or weak growth to promote a plant's health. But I'm most attentive to removing faded blooms daily to encourage plants to continue blooming and to prevent some plants, such as nicotiana and pansies, from going to seed. I deadhead by cutting or pinching below the flower pod, just above a node, rather than simply pulling the flower from its pod.

Taking tip cuttings for propagating plants is a great way to save money and grow more plants.

Grow Plants with Tip Cuttings

BY STEVE SILK

OVER THE YEARS I'VE PROPAGATED HUNDREDS of new coleus (*Solenostemon scutellarioides* cvs.) plants. Considering the vast number I use in my garden each year, I have to. Many of the varieties I want cannot be grown reliably from seed, and I just can't justify buying, say, 15 of the same plant at $5 a pop. So instead, I buy one and plunder it for tip cuttings, which I use to grow more plants. Within two weeks of returning home from a garden center with just the right coleus, I can root a whole colony of its offspring. Then I take tip cuttings from that brood, and soon I have a whole passel of plants.

And it doesn't stop with coleus. Propagating by tip cuttings works just as well with other tender perennials—those not typically hardy in cold temperatures —like flowering maples (*Abutilon* spp. and cvs.), geraniums (*Pelargonium* spp. and cvs.), sages (*Salvia* spp. and cvs.), and many more plants (see "Best Plants to Root," p. 192). As with hardy perennials, I'm dividing to multiply, but all I need is bits and pieces of the plant's stem and leaves rather than entire sections containing buds and roots, so if I spy a hard-to-find, must-have specimen in a friend's garden, I can ask for a tip cutting or two to try at home.

I take cuttings three times a year: in late spring or early summer, to increase my stock of plants; in late summer, to create plants to overwinter indoors; and in early spring, to grow new plants that will be ready for the garden when temperatures rise. Here are seven easy steps to successful tip cuttings.

Take tip cuttings, ensuring each piece has three sets of leaves.

Ready your pots

It's best to grow tip cuttings in a soilless potting mix containing perlite (a volcanic mineral), vermiculite (a micaceous mineral), or sand for good drainage. You can whip up your own mix by combining equal volumes of peat moss and perlite in a 5-gallon bucket, adding water, and stirring. The mix should be moist, but not soaked—just wet enough that if you squeeze a handful of medium, a few drops of water dribble out. After the mix is ready, fill your pots (I normally use 3-inch plastic containers) and gently tamp down the medium.

Make the cuts

For plants growing outdoors, take tip cuttings in the morning, when the plant's tissues are turgid. To ensure that tissues are well watered, give any candidates for cutting a good dousing the night before. Indoors, tip cuttings can be taken anytime. Use your trusty pruners to lop off stem tips, making sure that each piece

has at least three sets of leaves. The stem should not be too woody or too soft; it should snap when bent.

Prepare the cuttings

1. Working in a shady spot, begin by trimming off the bottom pair of leaves right at the stem using a clean razor blade, pruners, or a sharp pair of scissors.

2. Next, snip off the bottom of the stem just below where you removed the leaves. Leave the top two sets of leaves intact, unless they are very large, as with, say, angels' trumpets (*Brugmansia* spp. and cvs.). In this case, cut them in half crosswise so the foliage will lose less water.

3. Finally, dip the lower stem and the wounds where the leaves were removed into a small jar of rooting hormone, tapping any excess hormone on the stem back into the jar. Rooting hormone is reported to be nontoxic, but I like to wear latex gloves when working with any chemical.

Pot them up

1. Use a pencil to make a hole about an inch deep at the center of a prefilled pot. Then stick a cutting into the hole, taking care not to brush off the rooting hormone. Don't stick the cutting in too deep because those roots that touch the bottom of the container have a tendency to rot.

2. Next, firm up the soil around the cutting so that the plantlet stands tall and there's good contact between the stem and the potting mix. As you pot up the cuttings, transfer them to a tray.

3. When it's full, pour water into the tray to provide a good bottom watering. I leave about a quarter inch of excess water in the tray. Try to avoid watering from above, since water washing down through the soil carries away much of the rooting hormone.

Best Plants to Root

HERE ARE SOME tender perennials I've rooted with ease. It's worth trying this technique on almost any plant, provided the cutting has a bit of stem and several sets of leaves.

African daisy
Arctotis spp. and cvs.*

Alternanthera
Alternanthera spp. and cvs.

Angels' trumpet
Brugmansia spp. and cvs.

Cape fuchsia
Phygelius capensis

Coleus
Solenostemon scutellarioides cvs.

Cuphea
Cuphea spp. and cvs.

Flowering maple
Abutilon spp. and cvs.

Fuchsia
Fuchsia spp. and cvs.

Geranium
Pelargonium spp. and cvs.*

Helichrysum
Helichrysum spp. and cvs.*

Osteospermum
Osteospermum spp. and cvs.

Passionflower
Passiflora spp. and cvs.

Persian shield
Strobilanthes dyerianus

Plectranthus
Plectranthus spp. and cvs.

Redleaf hibiscus
Hibiscus acetosella

Salvia
Salvia spp. and cvs.*

Sanchezia
Sanchezia speciosa

Sweet potato vine
Ipomoea batatas cvs.

Tall verbena
Verbena bonariensis

Tropical smokebush
Euphorbia cotinifolia *

* Ventilation recommended

Essential Materials

Here's what you will need in order to get started.

- Shears or pruners
- Single-edge razor
- Pencil or pen
- Powdered or liquid rooting hormone
- Potting medium
- Pots
- Latex gloves (optional)

Provide optimum growing conditions

Most cuttings like a moist, enclosed environment safe from extremes of temperature, burning sun, drying winds, and pounding rain. I find the best place to grow many of my cuttings indoors is in a translucent plastic sweater box placed beneath fluorescent lights hanging an inch or so above the top. I place the cuttings in the inverted lid, with the bottom translucent part placed on top like a greenhouse dome. I slide an inexpensive heating pad—the kind made for seed starting—underneath the box. This setup, however, can be too humid for some kinds of cuttings, encouraging them to rot rather than root. In this case, for better ventilation, I use an old aquarium covered with a sheet of glass kept slightly askew so the setup can breathe a little. Outdoors, in summer, the process is easier. Just put a tray of cuttings in a shady spot.

Check for pests and diseases

Check your cuttings every few days to make sure the planting medium is moist and to look for pests. Any aphids or whiteflies should be sprayed with soapy water. Harsher insecticides could harm the fragile cuttings. Also remove any foliage that looks unhealthy or shows signs of fungal growth. If a plant continually sprouts fungal growth or seems to be rotting, it needs better ventilation.

Test for roots

Some plants root in 7 to 10 days; others may need a few weeks. To check if a cutting has rooted, tug on it gently. Sturdy resistance means it has roots. If it looks like a plant is not going to root, try a slightly larger cutting with a few more leaves. I've found geraniums, flowering maples, and tropical smokebush (*Euphorbia cotinifolia*) to be among the plants that do best with a slightly larger, leafier cutting. Another strategy for challenging plants is to take a cutting with a heel—a small strip of tissue from the main stem—at its base.

Once your cuttings have roots, allow them at least three days of increasing exposure to sun and wind before planting them in your garden.

ABOVE LEFT: In summer place cuttings on a tray outside in a shady spot.

ABOVE: Check for pests and diseases and remove any unhealthy growth.

Making your own potting soil allows you to customize the mix for different plants.

Make a Good Potting Soil

BY LEE REICH

I WORK HARD TO ENSURE THAT THE SOIL IN MY GARDEN is the best I can give my plants, and they reward me with robust health. Yet that same good soil if transferred to a container would cause the plants in it to languish. That's because garden soil doesn't offer enough air, water, or nutrients to a plant growing in a container. Potting soils are specifically formulated to overcome these limitations.

Potting soil needs to drain well but still hold moisture

One of the most important things a potting soil needs to do is provide roots access to air by letting water drain away from them. In the ground, the soil is usually deep enough to let excess water drain beyond root zones. In pots, however, water tends to accumulate at the bottom, despite drainage holes. The smaller the pore spaces of the soil in the pot, the higher that water layer will reach. Larger pores, formed by adding mineral aggregates to potting soils, readily admit water into the soil, then carry it through the medium and out the bottom. Then, all those large, empty spaces can fill with air.

Perlite, vermiculite, calcined clay (kitty litter), and sand are the mineral aggregates most commonly used in potting soils. Perlite and vermiculite are lightweight volcanic rocks naturally filled with air. I prefer perlite over the others because it does not decompose with time nor lose its aerating ability if the potting mix is compressed. Vermiculite is a valuable additive because it prevents some nutrients from leaching away, and it even provides a bit of potassium and magnesium.

A potting mix also must have ingredients that help it retain moisture. This is where organic materials—usually peat moss, sphagnum moss, or coir—come in. They cling to some of the water that the aggregates are helping to drain. Organic materials also hold on to nutrients that might otherwise wash away.

In addition to peat moss, vermiculite, and perlite, commercial mixes often contain sawdust or various grades of shredded bark. Lime may be added to help balance the acidity of the peat moss, and a small dose of fertilizer can often make up for the lack of nutrients.

Adding compost or garden soil can be beneficial

Most gardeners make potting soil by combining perlite or vemiculite with peat or sphagnum moss. Two other organic materials that you could add to your potting mix are leaf mold and compost, which offer a wide spectrum of nutrients.

Adding some garden soil to a home-made potting mix contributes bulk while buffering against pH changes and nutrient deficiencies. The reason that garden soil is rarely added to commercial mixes is because of the difficulty in obtaining a steady supply that is consistent in quality and free of toxins such as herbicide residues.

Soilless potting mixes are relatively free of living organisms, but mixes made with soil or compost are not. Some gardeners talk about "sterilizing" their potting mixes by baking them in the oven at high temperatures to rid the soil of harmful organisms, limiting the

Homemade Potting Soil Recipe

I'VE FOUND THAT MAKING MY OWN potting soil produces better results than commercial mixes and eliminates the need to monitor my containers' nutrient and pH levels. With plenty of good soil in my backyard, I have no trouble making this traditional potting medium. It features a mixed bag of ingredients, but I figure that plants, like humans, benefit from a varied diet. This mix can support plants for a year or two without additional fertilization.

I place a $1/2$-inch mesh screen over my garden cart and sift the peat moss, compost, and garden soil to remove any large particles. I then add the remaining ingredients and turn the materials over repeatedly with a shovel, adding water if the mix seems dry. After a few incantations, the stuff is ready to work its magic on everything from my tomato seedlings to my weeping fig.

Basic Recipe

Mix 2 gallons each of:
- peat moss
- perlite
- compost
- garden soil

with $1/2$ cup each of:
- dolomitic limestone
- soybean meal
- greensand
- rock phosphate
- kelp powder

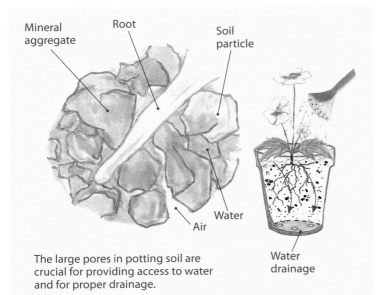

Mineral aggregate
Root
Soil particle
Air
Water
Water drainage

The large pores in potting soil are crucial for providing access to water and for proper drainage.

hazards of damping-off and other diseases. What I hope they mean is that they "pasteurize" their mixes. Heating homemade potting mixes to sterilizing temperatures wipes out all living things, beneficial and detrimental, leaving a clean slate for possible invasion of pathogens and causing nutritional problems such as ammonia toxicity. Pasteurization, which occurs at lower temperatures, kills only a fraction of the organisms. The best way to pasteurize your soil is to put it in a baking pan with a potato embedded in the soil. Bake it at 350°F for about 45 minutes. When the potato is cooked, the potting mix is ready.

I don't pasteurize my potting mix. I rely, instead, on healthy container-gardening practices such as timely watering, good air circulation, and adequate light to avoid disease problems. Beneficial micro-organisms in compost and garden soil also help fend off pests.

Soil Terms

THE FIRST STEP IN CREATING your own potting soil is understanding the roles of potential ingredients. Here is a glossary of some common soil terms.

Coarse Sand: Variably sized sand particles that improve drainage and add weight to soils.

Commercial Potting Soil: A variable mix of several ingredients, usually including peat moss, perlite, and vermiculite; can serve as a base for custom mixes.

Composted Cow Manure: Manure that has been aged for up to a year. Boosts nitrogen and loosens soil; also improves water retention.

Dolomitic Lime: Powdered limestone rich in magnesium carbonate; used to neutralize acidic soils.

Ground Pine Bark: Milled pine bark that retains moisture and improves aeration when included in soil mixes.

Peat Moss: Partially decomposed and milled mosses from boggy areas. Is slightly acidic and retains moisture.

Perlite: Volcanic mineral that has been expanded under high heat. Is lightweight and sterile, and improves water retention and aeration.

Slow-Release, Pelletized Fertilizer: Dry form of fertilizer that, when mixed into soil, releases nutrients slowly at each watering.

Vermiculite: Small bits of a micalike mineral that have been expanded under high heat. Retains moisture and improves aeration.

Healthy root system

Perlite

Water-absorbing gel

Composted pine bark

The Dirt on Soilless Mixes

BY JIM GARNER

THE TERM "POTTING SOIL" HAS BECOME SOMETHING of a misnomer in today's world of container gardening. Most bags of potting soil contain no field soil but are composed of a variety of organic and inorganic materials and are referred to as soilless mixes. As a commercial greenhouse operator and horticultural researcher, I've worked with all kinds of soilless mixes over the years that are far superior to soil-based mixes for a variety of reasons. If you have a clear understanding of the requirements for a good container medium and the various ingredients used in these products, choosing the right mix for your container plantings is in the bag.

Successful container gardening requires a potting medium that meets several of the plant's needs. The medium must be a stable reservoir of moisture and nutrients and remain loose enough to allow for root and water movement and the exchange of gases in the root zone. A growing medium must also have a pH (a measure of the alkalinity or acidity of a medium) that can support adequate nutrient uptake, and it must be free of soil-borne diseases, weed seeds, and toxins. Finally, it must adequately anchor and support the roots while still being heavy enough to provide sufficient ballast to prevent plants from tipping over. A well-blended soilless medium can easily do this without the problems and variability frequently encountered when field, or native, soils are used in containers.

With a good mix water will penetrate it quickly and drain freely from the bottom of the pot. When excess water has drained away, air will fill the large pore spaces, but enough water will be retained in the smaller spaces to provide ample moisture for the plant. In a poor mix, water may be slow to penetrate, the medium will become waterlogged, and a crust from algae or accumulated salts may form on the surface. Under these conditions, roots become starved for oxygen, plant growth slows, foliage may begin to yellow, and plants often succumb to root rot.

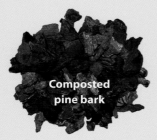

Composted pine bark

Coir

Sand

Vermiculite

Perlite

Organic ingredients hold water and nutrients

Some organic ingredients, such as peat moss, provide needed water-holding capacity, and others, like pine bark, can lend a porous structure to avoid compaction.

PEAT MOSS

The physical and chemical properties of peat moss make it an ideal base for most soilless mixes because it can hold both water and air. It's light, but its fibrous structure allows it to hold 15 to 20 times its weight in water. The peat fibers also give it a large amount of pore space (80 to 90 percent of its total volume). It holds nutrients well, and it readily shares them with the roots, thanks to its slightly acidic pH. Horticultural-grade peats come from the decomposed remains of sphagnum moss species that have accumulated over centuries in peat bogs. They are not a renewable resource, however, and concern about the sustainability of harvesting this product is a common topic of discussion among gardeners. Another type of peat that is used in soilless mixes is known as reed-sedge peat, but this material is generally inferior to sphagnum peat.

COMPOSTED PINE BARK

This material is a renewable resource and is one of the most widely used components in commercial container media, although barks from many other species are also processed for this purpose. Bark lacks the moisture-holding capacity of peat moss, so it can dramatically increase the porosity of a mix. Bark particles used in container media generally range in size from dustlike to about $3/8$ inch in diameter.

COIR

Another renewable organic material is coir, a derivative of coconut hulls that shows promise as a peat substitute. Coir has exceptional water-holding capacity, and when mixed with pine bark, it can eliminate or substantially reduce the need for peat moss in a mix. Other sources of organic matter that can be used in soilless mixes include composted manures, leaf mold, and crop residues such as rice hulls.

Inorganic ingredients improve drainage and add weight

Inorganic ingredients like sand, vermiculite, and perlite generally lend porosity to a mix. They can also help retain moisture and add weight or density.

SAND

This material can add needed weight to peat- and bark-based mixes and fill large pore spaces without impairing drainage. Coarse sand is preferred in most cases, and sand ground from granite is used in the best mixes. Fine sand with rounded grains, like that found at the beach, can actually reduce drainage when used in excessive amounts.

VERMICULITE

A mineral that has been heated until it expands into small accordion-shaped particles, vermiculite holds large amounts of air and water. But it can easily be compacted, so avoid packing down mixes containing large quantities of it. Vermiculite can also retain nutrients and help a mix resist changes in pH.

PERLITE

One of the more common ingredients in commercial potting mixes, perlite is an inert ingredient manufactured by heating a volcanic material to produce lightweight white particles. It promotes good drainage while holding nearly as much water as vermiculite. Other inorganic materials that are useful in potting media include polystyrene (plastic) beads and calcined clay, which is similar to kitty litter. Plastic beads are inert and serve only to promote drainage, but calcined-clay particles can actually improve the moisture- and nutrient-holding capacity of a mix.

Soilless mixes leave the fertilizing to you

Soilless mixes have little natural fertility, so they need fertilizer, lime, and sometimes other materials added to them to give the plants nutrients. Many soilless mixes contain a "starter charge" of fertilizer that can satisfy the nutritional requirements of plants for a few weeks, but longer-term fertility maintenance can require the addition of liquid fertilizers on a regular basis.

Another option is the application of a slow-release fertilizer, which provides a constant supply of available nutrients and can either be incorporated into the medium or simply top-dressed on the surface. The rate of nutrient release for most of these fertilizers is regulated by temperature, so plants receive more fertilizer when they are actively growing, and frequent watering will not leach the nutrients from the mix. Slow-release fertilizers are available in various formulations that can provide adequate nutrition for as short as three months or as long as two years.

Soilless mixes also have limited reserves of trace elements, so for best results, choose a fertilizer that also contains these micronutrients. Some mixes now come with slow-release fertilizers incorporated into the medium, and in these cases, the fertilizer analysis is usually included on the bag's label.

Most commercial mixes have ample lime added, so the pH should remain fairly stable over time. Soilless media perform well at a slightly acidic pH, so the lime requirements for these mixes

TIP

Don't Use Native Soil in Pots

Field soils can be appropriate for growing plants in the garden, but these soils are unsuited for growing plants in containers. In most cases, the texture of field soils is simply too fine to ensure adequate aeration in containers, and pots or planters of any size are generally too shallow to permit proper drainage. Soilless media have larger particles, which form bigger spaces or pores to hold air in the medium while still retaining enough water to allow plants to survive.

are not as critical as for native garden soils. When in doubt about the fertility of a soilless mix, a soil test may be useful, but be sure to indicate that you have an artificial or greenhouse medium when submitting your samples.

One positive trend in soilless media products is improved labeling on the bags. Many products now list all the ingredients and additives on the package (mixes with systemic insecticides added are always clearly labeled).

If you have an understanding of what components do in a mix, then choosing the right product for your container-gardening needs has never been easier.

Drip irrigation makes watering a cinch, thanks to hose and tubing that snakes among the containers, trickling water into them.

Drip Irrigation 101

BY STEVE SILK

THANKS TO A DROUGHT, I LOST A PASSEL OF PLANTS. But the biggest casualty was my free time. It seems as if I spent every available minute that summer on the patio with hose in hand, trickling water into the 50 or so parched pots that housed my favorite finds. Even during a rainy summer, container plants require a lot of watering and fertilizing. But that thirsty summer pushed me over the edge; I broke down and installed a drip-irrigation system for my containers.

I spent about $50 and several hours putting it all together, but the results—and the time it saves me daily—are worth far more. Drip irrigation is something I recommend to anyone who tends a lot of pots.

But before you plunge in, here's an important caveat: You'll want to use drip irrigation in a place where you'll be able to keep attendant water lines hidden from sight and out of the way of foot traffic, errant weed whackers, and lawn mowers. Because I display most of my plants against the south wall of the house, I hide the system between the wall and the containers. On a deck, you could run the water-supply lines beneath the decking and up through the cracks between boards.

Another concern was that I wanted a system that could meet the needs of all my plants, from water- and fertilizer-grubbing tropicals like *Brugmansia* and *Canna* cultivars to more self-reliant desert dwellers like *Echeveria* and *Agave* species and cultivars. And because my display changes during each season and from year to year, I needed an adaptable system so that I could move things about.

How to Build a Drip Irrigation System

Supplies You Will Need

ONE DRIP-IRRIGATION KIT FOR container plants may be all you need if you have municipal water and if your container plants have similar water requirements. Kits contain these basic materials:

- a device that couples the system to a hose bib

- a length of main hose 1/2 inch or so in diameter to pipe water throughout the collection

- figure-eight tubing for clamping the main hose

- sections of 1/4-inch-diameter feeder tubing to relay water from the main hose to the pots

- connectors to link lengths of tubing to the hose

- emitters to control the amount of water to pots

If your plants have diverse water requirements, you'll need a wider range of emitters than a single kit provides. You can mix components from different manufacturers.

For well water, you'll need a special filter to prevent debris from clogging the system.

A hose 1/2 inch or so in diameter pipes water throughout the designated area.

An emitter controls how much water actually gets delivered to a given pot.

A sprinkler-head emitter makes it possible to adjust water flow to a pot.

Punch holes for connectors.

Mount the emitters above the soil.

Add a T-connector to attach extra feeder tubes.

Fold and clamp the hose.

Step 1:
Setup is a snap

- **EXTEND THE HOSE.**
Run a length of the main hose from a water outlet to a point just beyond where you'll need water. Be generous; leave some extra hose at the end.

- **PUNCH HOLES IN THE HOSE.**
Use a hole punch or nail to perforate the main hose near any spot you want to put a pot.

- **ATTACH CONNECTORS.**
Plug a connector into each hole, and attach enough feeder tubing to reach the container. Size the feeder tubing generously so you can later move the pots a bit.

Step 2:
Get with the flow

- **SIZE THE EMITTERS.**
Emitters come in various capacities, including models that deliver 1/2 gph (gallons per hour), 1 gph, and 2 gph. Adjustable units can deliver up to 10 gph. There's also soaker tubing, which emits a specific amount of water for each foot of length.

- **SET A WATERING LEVEL.**
The level should serve your greatest number of containers. If most of your plants are of moderate thirst, you may want to outfit each with an emitter of middling capacity, say, a 2-gph emitter.

- **ADJUST THE SYSTEM.**
Desert plants might get a 1-gph or a 1/2-gph emitter each, while thirstier plantings, thanks to extra tubing and multiple outlet connectors (called T-connectors), might get multiple emitters. For the thirstiest plants, consider adjustable emitters, which can douse pots with up to 10 gph.

Monitor plantings and adjust the system as needed.

• **MOUNT THE EMITTERS.**
Use plastic stakes to raise emitters above the soil level to reduce the chance of clogging.

Step 3:
Adjust and monitor

• **FOLD AND CLAMP.**
Flush the debris out of your system, then fold and clamp the far end of the hose.

• **ASSESS THE FLOW.**
Turn the water back on, and let it flow until it comes out of the bottom of the moderately thirsty containers. Are the other pots getting too much water or too little? Modify by adding an emitter here, using a smaller capacity one there, or opening or closing the adjustable emitters a bit at a time.

• **KEEP AN EYE ON THINGS.**
Monitor the system for a week and fine-tune. If emitters or feeder tubes are popping off, the water pressure is too high. Most drip-system manufacturers sell devices that reduce water pressure.

• **FERTILIZE.**
Most drip systems can be equipped with a device that holds, dilutes, and delivers occasional food with the water.

Watering all of these pot-grown plants takes less than a minute, thanks to a well-concealed drip-irrigation system.

Thanks to all my hand watering in the past, I knew about how much water each pot needed. Armed with that basic information, I found that assembling my drip-irrigation system was as simple as snapping together a set of Tinkertoys®.

Once my system was in place, I was home free. I'd walk out back, flip on the water, and a half hour later I'd walk back and turn it off. Watering and fertilizing 50 containers took me less than a minute a day. Now that's low-maintenance gardening.

Spectacular Combination

1. **'The Line' coleus**
   Solenostemon scutellarioides 'The Line'
   ZONE: 11

2. **Feather grass**
   Stipa tenuissima
   ZONES: 7–11

3. **Diascia**
   Diascia cv.
   ZONES: 8–9

4. **Million bells**
   Calibrachoa cv.
   ANNUAL

5. **'Black Heart' sweet potato vive**
   Ipomoea batatas 'Black Heart'
   ZONE: 11

6. **Petunia**
   Petunia cv.
   ANNUAL

Build a Better Hanging Basket

BY C. DWAYNE JONES

H ANGING BASKETS CAN SERVE A VARIETY OF functions, from accenting a front porch to filling an empty wall. No matter what the purpose, they offer an opportunity to play with plant combinations to create a riot of color. Today's ever-shrinking landscapes mean fewer places to cultivate. Planting a hanging basket may be just the ticket for expanding your gardening realm. It is also one of the easiest ways to connect your garden with your home.

Trailing plants are traditionally used in hanging baskets with three plants of the same variety planted in the top. Another way to craft a hanging garden is to use an open-sided basket and plant the sides as well, a technique that allows me to use three to four times the number of plants in a traditional basket. I normally use a jumble of clumpers and trailers to create the illusion of masses of color and texture. I also mix in a few plants with great foliage to add interest throughout the growing season.

Stagger Your Plants

To ensure maximum coverage while preserving visibility, place plants in a checkerboard pattern. After spacing plants evenly in the bottom row, create the next row so that its plants fall between, not directly above, those below.

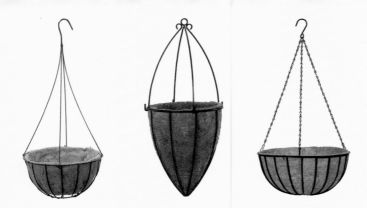

Baskets and liners come in myriad shapes and sizes.

Choose a basket

When it comes to baskets, size—or in this case, volume—does matter. The volume of the basket is directly related to the amount of water your hanging garden can retain; if you select a basket that is too small, you'll have to water daily, if not more often. A larger basket can make taller columns or posts look more in scale with your house or landscape. I use baskets that have open sides so that I can cut slits in the liner in a checkerboard pattern for planting.

Insert a liner

To fully cover large baskets, you may need to overlap two rectangular sections of liner. While the exact lengths depend on the size of your basket, allow enough extra material so that when the basket is filled with soil, some will still spill over the edges. Overlapping the liner in the bottom of the basket has the added benefit of slowing water flow out of the basket.

Build a base layer of potting soil

Start with a base layer of good-quality potting soil in the bottom of your basket. Press it against the bottom and sides of the basket so that you have a firm background to cut against when making the slits for the first row of plants. The soil level should be about 4 to 6 inches above the bottom of the basket when you complete this step.

Insert a water reservoir

To help with aeration and watering, I insert a vertical 8- to 10-inch section of slotted black drainpipe, available at any hardware store. I adjust the length so that 2 to 3 inches are exposed above the final soil level; this ensures that the drainpipe does not fill with potting soil during rainfall or waterings. I place the pipe so that the end sits about 4 to 5 inches above the bottom of the basket. If the drainpipe hits the bottom of the basket, water will simply drain right out of the basket instead of filling the surrounding area. The pipe directs the water toward the bottom of the basket, which is the first place to dry out.

Cut the liner and add plants

Using a sharp object, make small incisions in the liner just below the current soil level and carefully poke the root-balls of the plants through from the outside. Small plugs or cell pack–size annuals work best because they minimize the size of the openings in your liner; larger holes will let potting soil spill out and may even cause young plants to wash out during watering. If you must use larger plants, gently wash most of the potting soil from the root system and carefully compress the root mass into a torpedo shape and slip it through the liner.

Continue planting to the top

Keep adding layers of potting soil, cutting slits, and inserting rows of plants in a staggered pattern until you reach the top of the basket. Top off your planting with a few upright annuals or perhaps even some small grasses. Trim the liner to about 1 to 3 inches above the final soil level so that a small amount peeks over the edge of the basket. This reduces the chance of potting soil being washed out of the basket when watering. Then, give the whole basket a good soaking.

Liner Choices Abound

All of the popular liner choices have their pros and cons.

- Sphagnum moss is nice looking but is tedious to work with and offers limited water-holding capacity.

- Cocoa liners are attractive throughout the growing season, but they are thick, making it difficult to plant through the sides.

- Burlap liners, treated with copper to slow degradation, are thin but can be unattractive and retain almost no water.

- Supamoss, pictured, is a relatively new product that combines the best of both worlds. It is made of dyed, recycled cotton fibers that are sewn to thin green plastic sheeting. The tiny needle holes allow for water to drain, yet the plastic membrane conserves the majority of the water for the plants. It is easy to poke holes into this material for planting, and the green, mossy look is appealing.

Hypertufa looks like stone but weighs less and takes whatever shape you want.

Make Your Own Container

BY MICHELLE GERVAIS

T O ME, DESIRE, NOT NECESSITY, IS THE MOTHER OF invention. I don't need a stone trough. I just really want one. Unfortunately, they're not easy to come by, and when I do stumble upon one, I can't justify spending hundreds of dollars to buy it. Instead, I make my own out of hypertufa. Containers made from this substance are wonderful for displaying rock-garden plants or succulents. Over time, the hypertufa ages gracefully, collecting a patina of moss and lichen.

The process I use to mold containers is much simpler than the usual box-in-box method that sandwiches hypertufa and some metal mesh in a frame. Instead, I simply pack hypertufa around an overturned plastic container. And because it's so easy to work with, hypertufa can be molded into many sizes and shapes.

TIP

Enhance Your Container

To dress up your container, place evergreen sprigs or thick leaves around the rim of the mold before you start building the sides of your container. Lift them gently from the rim when you remove the mold.

Five Steps to a Hypertufa

TO STRENGTHEN POTS, I ADD A SMALL handful of synthetic concrete reinforcing fibers to each batch. They are easier to work with than sheets of wire mesh embedded in the hypertufa. You can find them at masonry-supply stores or online.

Supplies

- Mixing tub
- Container for measuring
- Peat moss
- Perlite
- Portland cement
- Concrete reinforcing fibers
- Dust mask
- Rubber gloves
- Trowel
- Plastic drop cloth
- Plastic container for making a mold
- Wire brush

The recipe

$1^{1}/_{2}$ parts sphagnum peat moss

$1^{1}/_{2}$ parts perlite

1 part Portland cement

Handful of concrete reinforcing fibers

Water

Step 1

Measure and mix the peat moss, perlite, cement, and reinforcing fibers in your tub. You'll kick up plenty of dust at this stage, so be sure to wear a dust mask.

Add a little water while stirring with a trowel. Test the consistency frequently; it's much easier to add water than it is to readjust the dry ingredients. When a squeezed handful retains its shape and doesn't release more than a few drops of water, the mix is ready.

Step 2

Mold the mixture around the chosen object, which has been placed upside down on the plastic drop cloth. Avoid using an object with a pronounced lip since it would be difficult to remove the object from the finished container.

Pack the mixture up around the sides of the object, tamping the mixture down firmly to bond the hypertufa to itself and to avoid a crumbly texture. A 1- to 2-inch-thick layer on all sides will create strong walls.

Flatten the intended bottom of the completely covered object for stability, and shape the sides to a desired form. Then poke your finger through the bottom to create a drainage hole.

Step 3

Wrap the container in the plastic drop cloth, and place it in a shady spot for about a day to let it harden.

Step 4

Remove the wrapping after the hypertufa has had a day to harden. The mixture will be firm but still soft enough to work with. Turn the container over, and remove the mold.

Brush the sharp edges and the smooth top, if desired, to give a rougher, more natural look to the container.

Step 5

Rewrap the container, and place it in a shady place for another two days. Then unwrap it and soak it with a hose periodically over the next few weeks to leach out the residual lime from the cement, which would harm plants.

Terra-cotta pots are available
in myriad shapes and styles.

A Gallery of Great Containers

BY FINE GARDENING EDITORS

CONTAINERS MAY BE THE OLDEST FORM OF GARDEN ornament, but right now, they're in, they're hot, and they're addictive. Once you begin collecting them, you will find it hard to discipline yourself. Rare is the container gardener who confines himself or herself to a few pots or even quite a few because the possibilities are limitless and so tempting.

You can choose from a variety of alluring shapes and materials: tall, graceful Victorian urns made of cast iron; classical earthenware oil jars; homey terra-cotta strawberry jars; and square or rectangular stone and cement troughs. Traditional flowerpot shapes remain a perennial favorite with gardeners because of their simplicity and practicality and are now available in everything from pottery to fiberglass.

There is no reason to be bound by convention. Some of the most amusing and attractive containers were originally intended for very different purposes. As long as there are enough holes for drainage, you can get away with using anything. But keep in mind that the size and material will affect how much watering is required. For example, small containers dry out faster than large ones, and water evaporates more quickly from porous materials than from nonporous materials.

Finally, don't forget color when it comes to choosing pots. Basically, there are two schools of thought. One maintains that the container should serve as a noncompetitive background for the plants. If you share this view, you will have no difficulty finding what you need at the nearest garden center, where a majority of the pots are made from neutral-toned clay or concrete. But you can also be adventurous and seek out glazed ceramic containers in gorgeous hues to either harmonize or contrast with the colors of plants. Either way, the photos in this section will give you plenty of ideas.

Glazed Ceramic

Treat glazed ceramic containers kindly and store them indoors in the winter. Fragile but fabulous, they offer a rainbow of colors and color combinations from restrained to over-the-top. On the left, a classic jar, glazed in silvery blue-violet, coordinates with foliage plants in the same color family. Above, artist Keeyla Meadows has pulled out all the stops with her own one-of-a-kind ceramic container, employing a lively palette of warm, bright pastels dominated by tints of pink and orange.

Limestone

Less expensive than solid limestone, dry-cast limestone vessels (facing page) mimic pots that have been around since Roman times. The natural color ranges from warm white to soft tan, but the material can either be tinted or the natural color altered with an applied wash. Suitable for all seasons, dry-cast limestone is frost-proof and withstands the ravages of weather year-round. Looking much less polished and truly as old as the hills, the container above was carved from blocks of limestone from the mountains of Mexico. Vessels like this one were originally used as watering troughs for livestock. While antique specimens are both rare and costly, modern copies are reasonably priced. Beautiful to look at but quite heavy to lift, they are tolerant of cold temperatures and can be left in situ during the winter, as long as the vessel has drainage holes in the bottom. Use a masonry bit if you need to drill holes.

Stone and Cement

You won't find a container like this
(on the facing page) at a garden center,
but you might be able to put together
something similar. In this lovely piece,
a hand-carved stone bowl rests on the
cement capital of a classical column;
both are supported by a fluted stone
base. Cold temperatures pose no threat
to either material, and they are visually
compatible because of their neutral tones
and weathered appearance.

Hypertufa

What looks like stone but weighs less, is
inexpensive, winter-hardy, and lasts for
years? Hypertufa, a do-it-yourself stone-
like material made from Portland cement
and lightened with sphagnum peat moss
and agricultural perlite. A small quantity
of shredded nylon fiber, available where
building supplies are sold, can be added
for strength. Mixed with water, the rather
stiff dough can be shaped over a form or
an armature of chicken wire.

Fiberglass

Fiberglass is more expensive than plastic but is worth it. Feather-light and durable, it is also flexible enough to give when the soil freezes and therefore can be left outdoors in the winter. Fiberglass can be molded into any shape and made to look like many materials, from stone to wood to metal.

Wood

The humble whiskey barrel, made from rot-resistant oak, has never lost its rustic charm. Averaging 24 inches across and 18 inches deep, a half barrel provides ample room for a canna surrounded by a strong supporting cast of marigolds and other annuals. Window boxes and planters made from cedar and redwood are also long lasting and can be stained, painted, or allowed to weather naturally to shades of gray.

Cast Iron

The most widely used of all the metals, iron has been made into tools, vessels, and utensils for thousands of years. Popular during the Victorian era, both cast and wrought iron can either be painted or allowed to rust to a rich brown, a hue that always looks at home in the natural landscape. The differ-ence between the two iron alloys is that cast iron contains a high proportion of carbon, which makes it too brittle to work, whereas wrought iron has a low carbon content and is malleable. All iron containers are heavy, but they need no protection from the elements and can remain in place year-round.

Sheet Metal and Galvanized Steel

These nontraditional metal containers are attractive and original. Only an imaginative gardener would think of filling an empty paint bucket with a sprightly clump of grass. Certainly, it took a sharp eye and a good sense of humor to see possibilities in the roof vent from an old chicken house (above). Karmin Mullins, a nurse and master gardener from Center Point, Iowa, lined her found container (right) with moss to hold in the soil and moisture. If your metal container is intact, drill holes in the bottom to allow for good drainage.

Iron and Steel

Iron and steel weather outdoors to a pleasing shade of reddish brown. On the left, horticulturist Dan Benarcik of Chanticleer, a public garden in Pennsylvania, has fashioned an interesting plant stand from rebar, a common steel rod used in reinforcing masonry.

The three triangular containers are made from flat sheets of punched metal. Above, narrow, upright plants are "contained" to intriguing effect by the rusted steel grid of an old cold-air return.

Terra-cotta

Terra-cotta, literally translated, means "baked earth." Raw clay can be thrown on a wheel or formed by hand, giving the potter great leeway in designing vessels. Gardeners favor terra-cotta for its gentle hues, which go with all flower and foliage colors and look natural in a garden setting. Some of the most beautiful terra-cotta pots are made in Italy from Tuscan clays.

The garden shown above contains a classic Ali Baba jar and strawberry pot. Heavy to ship and fragile to pack, imported pots are expensive and must be treated with care. Porous clay absorbs water from the soil, which expands when it freezes, causing pots to crack. In cold winter climates, be sure to empty all clay pots.

Modern Materials

LIGHTWEIGHT AND INEXPENSIVE, POTS MADE FROM MODERN SYNTHETIC MATERIALS LOOK like their traditional counterparts but have some advantages. You can move them easily, they weather well, and you can get almost any look you want. You have to watch how much you water because the pots are not porous, but these pots are unsurpassed for growing moisture-loving plants like ferns.

- **Composite and polyresin** pots are lightweight synthetic newcomers that replicate the look and texture of hand-carved stone, weathered and mossy concrete, or even the patina of old plaster, copper, or bronze. These pots are frost resistant and durable, and they provide some insulation at only a fraction of the cost of the real thing.

- **Foam or polystyrene** pots are lightweight, inexpensive, and nonporous. They come in many shapes and finishes. Their thick walls protect plants during cold winters and hot summers. Because they are lightweight, they may need to be weighed down or staked in windy sites.

- **Plastic pots** are lightweight, inexpensive, and hold moisture well. There are plastic pots to match almost any style, from beadboard to clay. Look for pots labeled as UV treated. They stand up to strong sunlight and won't overheat the soil and roots. These lightweight pots might also need weights or stakes in windy sites.

- **Rubber** has recently been recycled into flexible, nonporous pots that tolerate freezing and are heavy enough to withstand moderate winds without toppling.

Composite

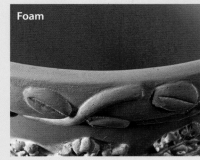

Foam

Rubber

The USDA Plant Hardiness Zone Map

The zones stated in *Fine Gardening* are based on several sources and should be treated as general guidelines when selecting plants for your garden. Many other factors may come into play in determining healthy plant growth. Microclimates, wind, soil type, soil moisture, humidity, snow, and winter sunshine may greatly affect the adaptability of plants. For more information and to zoom in on your area, visit the map online at www.usna.usda.gov/Hardzone/ushzmap.html.

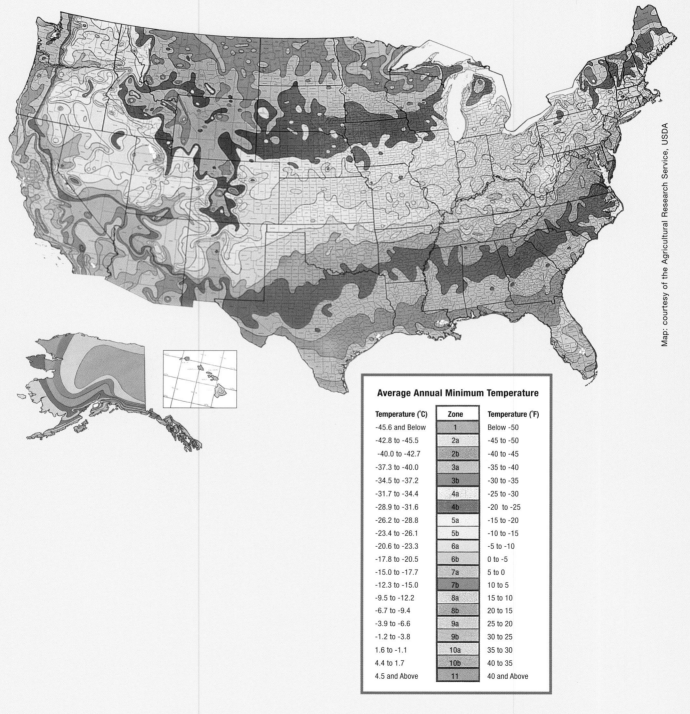

Map: courtesy of the Agricultural Research Service, USDA

Average Annual Minimum Temperature

Temperature (°C)	Zone	Temperature (°F)
-45.6 and Below	1	Below -50
-42.8 to -45.5	2a	-45 to -50
-40.0 to -42.7	2b	-40 to -45
-37.3 to -40.0	3a	-35 to -40
-34.5 to -37.2	3b	-30 to -35
-31.7 to -34.4	4a	-25 to -30
-28.9 to -31.6	4b	-20 to -25
-26.2 to -28.8	5a	-15 to -20
-23.4 to -26.1	5b	-10 to -15
-20.6 to -23.3	6a	-5 to -10
-17.8 to -20.5	6b	0 to -5
-15.0 to -17.7	7a	5 to 0
-12.3 to -15.0	7b	10 to 5
-9.5 to -12.2	8a	15 to 10
-6.7 to -9.4	8b	20 to 15
-3.9 to -6.6	9a	25 to 20
-1.2 to -3.8	9b	30 to 25
1.6 to -1.1	10a	35 to 30
4.4 to 1.7	10b	40 to 35
4.5 and Above	11	40 and Above

Contributors

Andrea Albert grows everything from dill to datura on her patio in Boynton Beach, Florida.

Sydney Eddison is the award-winning author of numerous books on gardening, and is a longtime contributor to *Fine Gardening* magazine.

Cynthia Eichengreen is the head gardener at a resort, where she creates gardens with unusual themes.

Muffin Evander designs containers in Hunt Valley, Maryland.

Christine Froehlich is a garden designer living in Sodus Point, New York, on the banks of Lake Ontario.

Jim Garner is an associate professor of horticulture at Horry-Georgetown Technical College in Myrtle Beach, South Carolina.

Michelle Gervais is associate editor of *Fine Gardening* magazine and designs and maintains up to two dozen containers each season in her New Milford, Connecticut, garden.

Richard Hartlage is the author of *Bold Visions for the Garden*.

June Hutson is the supervisor of the Kemper Home Demonstration Gardens at the Missouri Botanical Garden.

C. Dwayne Jones is a horticulturist and the superintendent of parks and horticulture in Waynesboro, Virginia.

Gary R. Keim is a garden designer based in Lansdowne, Pennsylvania.

Juanita Nye surrounds her home in Portland, Oregon, with bountifully planted containers.

Tom Peace grows more than 50 different water-misers in his Texas and Colorado gardens.

Lee Reich, author of *The Pruning Book*, is a soil scientist who gardens in New Paltz, New York.

Dennis Schrader, co-author of *Hot Plants for Cool Climates*, is co-owner of Landcraft Environments in Mattituck, New York.

Andrew Schulman is a landscape designer who collects old roses for his garden in Seattle, Washington.

Steve Silk tends his diverse collection of container plantings in Farmington, Connecticut.

Greg Speichert, coauthor of *Encyclopedia of Water Garden Plants*, lives in northwest Indiana.

Joseph Tomocik is always on the lookout for new containers that he can turn into water gardens.

Credits

Credits

p. 24: Photo by Lee Anne White; Design: Gary Keim for a garden in Pennsylvania

p. 26: Photo by Michelle Gervais, courtesy *Fine Gardening*, © The Taunton Press, Inc.; Design: Denver Botanic Garden, Denver, Colorado

p. 27: (top) Photo by Michelle Gervais, courtesy *Fine Gardening*, © The Taunton Press, Inc.; (bottom) Photo by Jennifer Benner, courtesy *Fine Gardening*, © The Taunton Press, Inc.; Design: Denny Kidder for his garden, Newport, Kentucky

p. 28: (left) Photo by Todd Meier, courtesy *Fine Gardening*, © The Taunton Press, Inc.; Design: The Chicago Botanic Garden, Chicago, Illinois; (right) Photo by Michelle Gervais, courtesy *Fine Gardening*, © The Taunton Press, Inc.; Design: Tom Peace for a garden, Denver, Colorado

p. 29: Photo by Sydney Eddison; Design: Sydney Eddison

p. 30: Photo by Michelle Gervais, courtesy *Fine Gardening*, © The Taunton Press, Inc.; Design: Laura Crockett for her garden, Hillsboro, Oregon

p. 32: Photo by Virginia Small, courtesy *Fine Gardening*, © The Taunton Press, Inc.; Design: Gordon Hayward for his garden, Putney, Vermont

p. 33: Photos by Stephanie Fagan, courtesy *Fine Gardening*, © The Taunton Press, Inc.; Design: George Schoellkopf for Hollister House, Washington, Connecticut

p. 34: (top) Photo by Jennifer Benner, courtesy *Fine Gardening*, © The Taunton Press, Inc.; Design: Laura Crockett for her garden, Hillsboro, Oregon; (bottom) Photo by Todd Meier, courtesy *Fine Gardening*, © The Taunton Press, Inc.; Design: Gordon Hayward for his garden, Putney, Vermont

p. 35: (top) Photo by Todd Meier, courtesy *Fine Gardening*, © The Taunton Press, Inc.; Design: Nancy Goodwin for her garden, Hillsborough, North Carolina; (bottom) Photos by Stephanie Fagan, courtesy *Fine Gardening*, © The Taunton Press, Inc.; Design: Wesley Rouse for his garden, Southbury, Connecticut

p. 36: Photo by Todd Meier, courtesy *Fine Gardening*, © The Taunton Press, Inc.; Design: Donald Robertson of Town and Country Gardens for a rooftop garden, New York City

p. 38: (top) Photo by Jennifer Benner, courtesy *Fine Gardening*, © The Taunton Press, Inc.; Design: Sean Hogan for the town of Lake Oswego, Oregon; (bottom) Photo by Photo by Steve Silk; Design: Sydney Eddison for her garden, Newtown, Connecticut

p. 39: (top) Photo by Mary Carolyn Pindar; Design: Ryan Gainey for his garden, Decatur, Georgia; (bottom) Photo by Todd Meier, courtesy *Fine Gardening*, © The Taunton Press, Inc.; Design: Donald Robertson of Town and Country Gardens for a rooftop garden, New York City

p. 40: Photo by Staff of *Fine Gardening*, © The Taunton Press, Inc.

p. 42: Photo by Staff of *Fine Gardening*, © The Taunton Press, Inc.

p. 43: Photo © Allan Mandell

p. 44: Photo by Steve Silk

p. 45: Photo by Staff of *Fine Gardening*, © The Taunton Press, Inc.

p. 46: Photo by Michelle Gervais, courtesy *Fine Gardening*, © The Taunton Press, Inc.

p. 48: (bottom left) Photo by Todd Meier, courtesy *Fine Gardening*, © The Taunton Press, Inc.; (bottom middle) Photo by Lee Anne White; (bottom right) Photo by Stephanie Fagan, courtesy *Fine Gardening*, © The Taunton Press, Inc.

p. 49: (top left) Photo by Jennifer Brown; (top middle) Photo by Kathy Diemer; (top right, bottom left and bottom middle) Photos by Todd Meier, courtesy *Fine Gardening*, © The Taunton Press, Inc.; (bottom right) Photo by Michelle Gervais, courtesy *Fine Gardening*, © The Taunton Press, Inc.

p. 50: Photo by Jennifer Brown

p. 53: (top) Photo by Jennifer Benner, courtesy *Fine Gardening*, © The Taunton Press, Inc.; (bottom) Photo by Michelle Gervais, courtesy *Fine Gardening*, © The Taunton Press, Inc.

p. 54: Photos by Michelle Gervais, courtesy *Fine Gardening*, © The Taunton Press, Inc.

p. 55: (top) Photo by Jennifer Brown; (top middle and bottom) Photos by Jennifer Benner, courtesy *Fine Gardening*, © The Taunton Press, Inc.; (middle and bottom middle) Photos by Michelle Gervais, courtesy *Fine Gardening*, © The Taunton Press, Inc.

pp. 56–57: Photos by Michelle Gervais, courtesy *Fine Gardening*, © The Taunton Press, Inc.

p. 58: Photo by Allan Mandell

p. 60: Photo by Allan Mandell

p. 61: Photo by Jennifer Benner, courtesy *Fine Gardening*, © The Taunton Press, Inc.

pp. 62–63: Photos by Allan Mandell

pp. 64–65: Photos by Melonie Ice

p. 66: Photo by Michelle Gervais, courtesy *Fine Gardening*, © The Taunton Press, Inc.

p. 67: Photo by Linda Brown

p. 68: Photo by Danny Ewert

p. 69: Photo by Steve Nowotarski

p. 70: Photo by Sheila Gamble

p. 71: Photo by Debra Corrington

p. 72: Photo by Michelle Gervais, courtesy *Fine Gardening*, © The Taunton Press, Inc.

p. 74: Photo by Michelle Derviss

p. 75: Photo by Cheryl Thole

p. 76: Photo by Sandra Wagoner

p. 77: Photo by Motria Caudill

p. 78: Photo by Pam and Kevin Watkins

p. 79: Photo by Holly Buss

pp. 80, 82–84: Photos by Staff of *Fine Gardening*, © The Taunton Press, Inc.

p. 86: (top) Photo by Staff of *Fine Gardening*, © The Taunton Press, Inc.; (bottom) Photo by Susan A. Roth

p. 87: Photo by Staff of *Fine Gardening*, © The Taunton Press, Inc.

p. 88: Photo by Dennis Schrader

p. 90: Photo by Staff of *Fine Gardening*, © The Taunton Press, Inc.

p. 91: Photo by Dennis Schrader

p. 92: Photo by Staff of *Fine Gardening*, © The Taunton Press, Inc.

p. 94: Photos by Staff of *Fine Gardening*, © The Taunton Press, Inc.

p. 95: (top) Photo by Staff of *Fine Gardening*, © The Taunton Press, Inc.; (bottom) Photo by Susan A. Roth

p. 96: Photo by Steve Aitken, courtesy *Fine Gardening*, © The Taunton Press, Inc., Design: Muffin Evander, Hunt Valley, Maryland

p. 98: (left) Photo by Jennifer Benner, courtesy *Fine Gardening*, © The Taunton Press, Inc., Design: Sean Hogan for the town of Lake Oswego, Oregon; (right) Photo by Melissa Lucas, Design: Longwood Gardens, Kennett Square, Pennsylvania

pp. 100–105: Photos by Steve Aitken, courtesy *Fine Gardening*, © The Taunton Press, Inc.

pp. 106, 109–111, and 113: Photos by Staff of *Fine Gardening*, © The Taunton Press, Inc.

p. 114: Photo by Colleen Fitzpatrick, Design: the staff of Minter Gardens, Chilliwack, British Columbia

p. 116: Photo by Jennifer Benner, courtesy *Fine Gardening*, © The Taunton Press, Inc., Design: Danielle Ferguson, Ferguson's Fragrant Nursery, St. Paul, Oregon

p. 117: Photo by Todd Meier, courtesy *Fine Gardening*, © The Taunton Press, Inc., Design: Nancy Goodwin, Hillsborough, North Carolina

p. 118: Photo by Colleen Fitzpatrick, Design: Tom Hobbs, Vancouver, British Columbia

p. 119: Photo by Colleen Fitzpatrick, Design: the staff of Minter Gardens, Chilliwack, British Columbia

p. 120: (top) Photo by Melissa Lucas, Design: Nancy Ondra, Pennsburg, Pennsylvania; (bottom) Photo by Todd Meier, courtesy *Fine Gardening*, © The Taunton Press, Inc., Design: Nancy Goodwin, Hillsborough, North Carolina

p. 121: Photo by Michelle Gervais, courtesy *Fine Gardening*, © The Taunton Press, Inc.; Design: Gordon Hayward, Walpole, New Hampshire

p. 122: Photo by Jennifer Benner, courtesy *Fine Gardening*, © The Taunton Press, Inc., Design: the staff of the Chadwick Arboretum, Columbus, Ohio

p. 123: Photo by Michelle Gervais, courtesy *Fine Gardening*, © The Taunton Press, Inc.; Design: gardener, Bloomfield Hills, Michigan

p. 124: Photo by Steve Silk, Design: Jerry Fritz, Ottsville, Pennsylvania

p. 125: Photo by Michelle Gervais, courtesy *Fine Gardening*, © The Taunton Press, Inc.; Design: Scott Endres, St. Paul, Minnesota

p. 126: Photo by Michelle Gervais, courtesy *Fine Gardening*, © The Taunton Press, Inc.; Design: a home in Charleston, South Carolina

p. 127: Photo by Michelle Gervais, courtesy *Fine Gardening*, © The Taunton Press, Inc.; Design: Chris Kelley, Piasa, Illinois

Part 2: Great Plants

p. 128: (left) Photo by Allan Mandell; (middle) Photo by Jennifer Brown; (right) Photo courtesy Jackson & Perkins

p. 129: (left) Photo courtesy Avant Gardens; (middle) Photo courtesy Renee's Garden; (right) Photo courtesy www.proven winners.com

pp. 130, 132–135: Photos by Steve Aitken, courtesy *Fine Gardening*, © The Taunton Press, Inc.

pp. 136, 138–139: Photos by Richard Hartlage

p. 140: Photo © J. Paul Moore

pp. 142–143: Photos courtesy Antique Rose Emporium

pp. 144, 146–147: Photos by Jennifer Brown

pp. 148, 150–154: Photos by Steve Aitken, courtesy *Fine Gardening*, © The Taunton Press, Inc.

p. 155: Photo by Jerry Paiva

p. 156: Photo by Michelle Gervais, courtesy *Fine Gardening*, © The Taunton Press, Inc.; Design: Janet Gauthier, Michigan State University Radiology Garden, East Lansing, Michigan

p. 158: Photo by Jennifer Benner, courtesy *Fine Gardening*, © The Taunton Press, Inc.

p. 159: Photo by Michelle Gervais, courtesy *Fine Gardening*, © The Taunton Press, Inc.; Design: Catharine Heller, Toledo Botanical Garden, Toledo, Ohio

p. 160: Photo by Steve Aitken, courtesy *Fine Gardening*, © The Taunton Press, Inc.; Design: Steve Silk, Farmington, Connecticut; inset photos: (left) Photo courtesy www.provenwinners.com; (middle) Photo by Janet Jemmott, courtesy *Fine Gardening*, © The Taunton Press, Inc.; (right) Photo by Jennifer Benner, courtesy *Fine Gardening*, © The Taunton Press, Inc.

p. 162: (top) Photo by Michelle Gervais, courtesy *Fine Gardening*, © The Taunton Press, Inc.; (bottom) Photo by Michelle Gervais, courtesy *Fine Gardening*, © The Taunton Press, Inc., Design: Mike Holloway, the Denver Botanic Gardens, Denver, Colorado

p. 163: Photo by Todd Meier, courtesy *Fine Gardening*, © The Taunton Press, Inc., Design: the staff at the Chicago Botanic Garden, Glencoe, Illinois

p. 164: Photo courtesy White Flower Farm

p. 165: Photo by Jennifer Benner, courtesy *Fine Gardening*, © The Taunton Press, Inc.; Design: James Pickett, the VanDusen Botanical Garden, Vancouver, British Columbia

p. 166: Photos courtesy www.proven winners.com

p. 167: (top) Photo courtesy Singing Springs Nursery; (bottom) Photo courtesy www.provenwinners.com

p. 168: Photo courtesy www.proven winners.com

p. 169: (top left) Photo by Jennifer Benner, courtesy *Fine Gardening*, © The Taunton Press, Inc.; (top right) Photo by Jennifer Brown; (bottom left) Photo by Melissa Lucas; (bottom right) Photo by Stephanie Fagan, courtesy *Fine Gardening*, © The Taunton Press, Inc.

p. 170: (top) Photo courtesy Avant Gardens; (bottom) Photo courtesy White Flower Farm

p. 171: Photo courtesy Jackson & Perkins

pp. 172–173: Photos courtesy www.provenwinners.com

pp. 174–176: Photos by Michelle Gervais, courtesy *Fine Gardening*, © The Taunton Press, Inc.

p. 177: Photo courtesy White Flower Farm

p. 178: Photo by Melissa Lucas, Design: Roger Davis, Longwood Gardens, Kennett Square, Pennsylvania

p. 179: Photo courtesy Burpee

Part 3: Materials & Techniques

p. 180: (left) Photo by Steve Aitken, courtesy *Fine Gardening*, © The Taunton Press, Inc.; (middle) Photo by Michelle Gervais, courtesy *Fine Gardening*, © The Taunton Press, Inc.; (right) Photo by Todd Meier, courtesy *Fine Gardening*, © The Taunton Press, Inc., Design: Todd Meier for his garden, Ridgefield, Connecticut

p. 181: (left) Photo by Jennifer Benner, courtesy *Fine Gardening*, © The Taunton Press, Inc.; (middle) Photo by Michelle Gervais, courtesy *Fine Gardening*, © The Taunton Press, Inc.; (right) Photo by Steve Aitken, courtesy *Fine Gardening*, © The Taunton Press, Inc.

pp. 182–187: Photos by Staff of *Fine Gardening*, © The Taunton Press, Inc.

pp. 188–193: Photos by Virginia Small, courtesy *Fine Gardening*, © The Taunton Press, Inc.

pp. 194 & 196: Photos by Steve Aitken, courtesy *Fine Gardening*, © The Taunton Press, Inc.

p. 198: Photo by Scott Phillips, courtesy *Fine Gardening*, © The Taunton Press, Inc.

p. 200: Photos by Steve Aitken, courtesy *Fine Gardening*, © The Taunton Press, Inc.

p. 202: Photo by Michelle Gervais, courtesy *Fine Gardening*, © The Taunton Press, Inc

p. 204: (top) Photos by Virginia Small, courtesy *Fine Gardening*, © The Taunton Press, Inc., except bottom right: Photo by Jennifer Benner, courtesy *Fine Gardening*, © The Taunton Press, Inc.; (bottom left) Photo by Steve Aitken, courtesy *Fine Gardening*, © The Taunton Press, Inc.; (bottom) Photo by Virginia Small, courtesy *Fine Gardening*, © The Taunton Press, Inc.

p. 205: (top left) Photo by Michelle Gervais, courtesy *Fine Gardening*, © The Taunton Press, Inc.; (top right) Photo by Virginia Small, courtesy *Fine Gardening*, © The Taunton Press, Inc.

p. 206: Photo by Stephanie Fagan, courtesy *Fine Gardening*, © The Taunton Press, Inc.

p. 208: (top) Photos courtesy Bestnest; (middle right, bottom left & bottom right) Photos by Steve Aitken, courtesy *Fine Gardening*, © The Taunton Press, Inc.

p. 209: Photos by Steve Aitken, courtesy *Fine Gardening*, © The Taunton Press, Inc.

pp. 210–211: Photo by Michelle Gervais, courtesy *Fine Gardening*, © The Taunton Press, Inc.

pp. 212–213: Photos by Steve Aitken, courtesy *Fine Gardening*, © The Taunton Press, Inc.

p. 214: Photo by Jennifer Benner, courtesy *Fine Gardening*, © The Taunton Press, Inc., Design: Laura Crockett for her garden, Hillsboro, Oregon

p. 216: Photo by Stephanie Fagan, courtesy *Fine Gardening*, © The Taunton Press, Inc., Design: Fran Lenich for her garden, Wilton, Connecticut

p. 217: Photo by Virginia Small, courtesy *Fine Gardening*, © The Taunton Press, Inc., Design: Keeyla Meadows for her garden, Albany, California

p. 218: Photo by Jennifer Benner, courtesy *Fine Gardening*, © The Taunton Press, Inc., Design: the staff at Timberline Gardens, Arvada, Colorado

p. 219: Photo by Jennifer Benner, courtesy *Fine Gardening*, © The Taunton Press, Inc., Design: the staff at the Indianapolis Museum of Art, Indianapolis, Indiana

p. 220: Photo by Jennifer Benner, courtesy *Fine Gardening*, © The Taunton Press, Inc., Design: Barbara Bockbrader, Campo de Fiori, Sheffield, Massachusetts

p. 221: Photo by Michelle Gervais, courtesy *Fine Gardening*, © The Taunton Press, Inc., Design: Tom Nelson and Randy Bolin for their garden, Oakland, California

p. 222: Photo by Todd Meier, courtesy *Fine Gardening*, © The Taunton Press, Inc., Design: Todd Meier for his garden, Ridgefield, Connecticut

p. 223: Photo by Colleen Fitzpatrick, Design: the staff at Minter Gardens, Chilliwack, British Columbia

p. 224: Photo by Michelle Gervais, courtesy *Fine Gardening*, © The Taunton Press, Inc., Design: Tom Peace for a garden, Denver, Colorado

p. 225: (top) Photo by Karmin Mullins, Design: Karmin Mullins for her garden, Center Point, Iowa; (bottom) Photo by Jennifer Benner, courtesy *Fine Gardening*, © The Taunton Press, Inc., Design: Nancy Ondra for her garden, Pennsburg, Pennsylvania

p. 226: Photo by Jennifer Benner, courtesy *Fine Gardening*, © The Taunton Press, Inc., Design: Dan Benarcik of Chanticleer, Wayne, Pennsylvania

p. 227: Photo by Jennifer Benner, courtesy *Fine Gardening*, © The Taunton Press, Inc., Design: Laura Crockett, Hillsboro, Oregon

p. 228: Photo by Stephanie Fagan, courtesy *Fine Gardening*, © The Taunton Press, Inc., Design: Wesley Rouse for his garden, Southbury, Connecticut

p. 229: Photos © Donna Chiarelli

Index

Index note: page references in *italics* indicate a photograph; page references in **bold** indicate an illustration.

Index